Love you Ave

Grandma

WORRY
LESS,
PRAY
MORE

A TEEN GIRL'S DEVOTIONAL GUIDE
TO ANXIETY-FREE LIVING

JOANNE SIMMONS

WORRY LESS, PRAY MORE

A TEEN GIRL'S DEVOTIONAL GUIDE TO ANXIETY-FREE LIVING

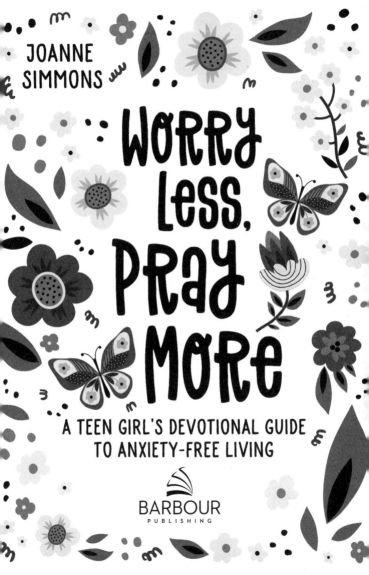

BARBOUR
PUBLISHING

Scripture quotations marked NIV are taken from the HOLY BIBLE, NEW INTERNATIONAL VERSION®. NIV®. Copyright © 1973, 1978, 1984, 2011 by Biblica, Inc.™ Used by permission. All rights reserved worldwide.

Scripture quotations marked NLV are taken from the New Life Version copyright © 1969 and 2003 by Barbour Publishing, Inc., Uhrichsville, Ohio, 44683. All rights reserved.

Scripture quotations marked NLT are taken from the *Holy Bible.* New Living Translation copyright© 1996, 2004, 2015 by Tyndale House Foundation. Used by permission of Tyndale House Publishers, Inc. Carol Stream, Illinois 60188. All rights reserved.

Scripture quotations marked CEV are from the Contemporary English Version, Copyright © 1995 by American Bible Society. Used by permission.

Scripture quotations marked ICB are from the Holy Bible, International Children's Bible® Copyright© 1986, 1988, 1999, 2015 by Thomas Nelson. Used by permission.

Published by Barbour Publishing, Inc., 1810 Barbour Drive, Uhrichsville, Ohio 44683, www.barbourbooks.com

Our mission is to inspire the world with the life-changing message of the Bible.

Member of the
Evangelical Christian
Publishers Association

Printed in China.

INTRODUCTION

"Do not worry about your life."
MATTHEW 6:25 NIV

Jesus said it straightforwardly—we're *not* supposed to worry about our lives. *Ha!* We might laugh at that. We might be thinking, *But Jesus didn't live my life! And He doesn't know how hard things are for me!* But then we need to remember exactly who Jesus is—the holy one of God. If Jesus said it, we should try our very best to obey it. And we should remember that He "understands our weaknesses, for he faced all of the same testings we do, yet he did not sin" (Hebrews 4:15 NLT). So how do we strive to obey Jesus' command to not worry? We "go with complete trust to the throne of God. We will receive His loving-kindness and have His loving-favor to help us whenever we need it" (Hebrews 4:16 NLV). Worry *less* and pray *more*, girl!

SHAPE YOUR WORRIES INTO PRAYERS

Don't fret or worry. Instead of worrying, pray.
Let petitions and praises shape your worries into
prayers, letting God know your concerns. Before
you know it, a sense of God's wholeness, everything
coming together for good, will come and settle
you down. It's wonderful what happens when
Christ displaces worry at the center of your life.
PHILIPPIANS 4:6–7 MSG

What worries are swirling in your mind today? Can you feel them churning in your chest and stomach too? Are they causing you to lose sleep? God cares when you're struggling with worries. He wants to take them away and give you His peace instead. Take a minute to imagine holding all your worries in your hands. Now use your hands to squeeze and mold those thoughts as you focus on God and His goodness. Praise Him. Ask Him for whatever you need. Soon you'll have shaped those worries into something completely new, something totally good—they'll be transformed into prayers, which will draw you closer to God and His awesome love for you.

Dear God, please help me turn my worries into
prayer. I need Your peace—that sense of wholeness,
that reassurance that everything will come
together for good—to settle me down. Amen.

BECAUSE HE CARES FOR YOU

Cast all your anxiety on him because he cares for you.
1 Peter 5:7 NIV

The word *cast* in this version of this scripture is a good one. God doesn't mind one bit if you throw your anxiety at Him as hard as you can. He will catch your anxiety and destroy it. He loves you so much that He doesn't want you caught up in worries, wringing your hands and pacing the floor. He wants you to trust in His care. He wants you to be full of His peace. First Peter 5:6 (NIV) says, "Humble yourselves, therefore, under God's mighty hand, that he may lift you up in due time." Hang in there as you wait for God to act in the situations that have you worried. Stay humble (not prideful), knowing that He is in control and He will lift you up according to His perfect plans and timing.

Dear God, I'm throwing my anxiety at You as hard as I can. Please get rid of it. Thank You for being such a good Father who wants to fill me with Your peace. I trust You will lift me up and out of the situations that worry me most. Amen.

JOY, PRAYER, AND GRATITUDE

Always be joyful. Never stop praying.
Be thankful in all circumstances, for this is God's
will for you who belong to Christ Jesus.
1 Thessalonians 5:16–18 nlt

This scripture is a great way to overcome anxiety. Can you focus on joy? How much are you praying these days? What do you have to be grateful for? Thinking about these things will help you remember the many ways God has already blessed you in life and will help you trust Him for the future—no matter what situations you're going through. Joy, constant prayer, and gratitude are God's will for those who belong to Jesus! When your mind and heart are full of those things, there won't be much room left for worries!

Dear God, I'm grateful You don't ever get tired of my prayers. Please help me to focus on joy, prayer, and gratitude to push all worry right out of my mind. Amen.

WHY DO WE WORRY?

God sent His Son to pay for our sins.
1 John 4:10 NLV

Do you ever wonder why worry is even a thing? We'd have nothing to worry about if sin didn't affect every part of life. When the first two people God created, Adam and Eve, chose to sin, it spread to all people after them—and sin brought hardship and worry and death to the world. But God made a way to overcome sin and experience life that lasts forever through a relationship with Him. He showed what incredible love He has for people by sending His one and only Son, Jesus Christ, to die to pay the price of sin for every single person. And then Jesus rose back to life, proving God's power over death—power that He gives to us when we accept Jesus as the Savior from our sin.

The very best prayer anyone can ever pray is a prayer of salvation, like this:

Dear God, I know that I make bad choices sometimes. Those things are sin, and I am a sinner. Please forgive me. I trust that You sent Your Son, Jesus Christ, as the only Savior from sin. I believe Jesus died on the cross to pay for my sin and rose again and gives me life that lasts forever. I want to give my life to You, God, and want to do my best to live like Jesus. I love You, and I need Your help in all things. Amen.

CONSTANT CONVERSATION

For we know how dearly God loves us, because he has given us the Holy Spirit to fill our hearts with his love.
ROMANS 5:5 NLT

When Jesus rose from the dead, He didn't stay on the earth. He went to heaven to be with God, but He didn't leave us alone. He gave us the Holy Spirit to be with us until He returns to earth again. When we believe in Jesus as Savior, the Holy Spirit lives in us, helping us and guiding us. So, as you pray, you can think about how all your thoughts are like a constant conversation with God. Let His nonstop presence comfort you and strengthen you as you endlessly talk to Him and ask for His help.

Dear God, help me to remember that You are always with me through the Holy Spirit. You want me to talk to You about anything and everything. I need Your help with that, God. I'm so grateful for Your gifts. Amen.

DEVOTE YOURSELF TO PRAYER

Devote yourselves to prayer,
being watchful and thankful.
COLOSSIANS 4:2 NIV

While you should think of prayer as constant conversation with God, it's important to have set, focused times of prayer too. You might already be doing this, and that's great. If so, keep it up!

Whatever your times of prayer are, you can always develop them even more. Right now, if you're remembering to say thanks to God for the food at each meal, also start telling Him other things you're thankful for that happened during the day. At night, if you're thanking Him for the day and asking for a good night's sleep, also ask Him for help with the things you'll be doing the next day and the problems that you and your loved ones are facing. Whatever you're talking to God about and whenever you're praying, keep increasing it. Ask for more faith in Him and for more of His help in your life and for His will to be done. You'll be growing closer and closer to your loving heavenly Father and experiencing more of His love and power as you do!

Dear God, please help me to be devoted to prayer. Help
me want to keep talking to You more and more! Amen.

THE SPIRIT OF TRUTH

*"When the Spirit of truth comes, he will guide you
into all truth. He will not speak on his own but will
tell you what he has heard. He will tell you about
the future. He will bring me glory by telling you
whatever he receives from me. All that belongs
to the Father is mine; this is why I said, 'The Spirit
will tell you whatever he receives from me.' "*
JOHN 16:13–15 NLT

Jesus said these words to His disciples, and the same
Spirit of truth is in you today if you have accepted Jesus
as your Savior. When worries feel like they are making
you crazy, remember that the Spirit is right there with
you, ready and willing to guide you into all truth. And the
truth about your worries is that they are never too big
for God to handle. He loves you and wants to help you
with them. Give your worries to Him, and then let Him
act on your behalf.

*Dear Jesus, thank You for being right here
with me through the Holy Spirit. Please help
me not to be guided by my worries but guided
by Your perfect truth instead. Amen.*

BESTSELLING BOOK OF ALL TIME

*All Scripture is inspired by God and is useful to teach
us what is true and to make us realize what is wrong
in our lives. It corrects us when we are wrong and
teaches us to do what is right. God uses it to prepare
and equip his people to do every good work.*

2 TIMOTHY 3:16–17 NLT

Do you know how popular the Bible is? *Guinness World
Records* says this: "The best-selling book of all time is the
Christian Bible. It is impossible to know exactly how many
copies have been printed in the roughly 1500 years since
its contents were standardized, but research conducted
by the British and Foreign Bible Society in 2021 suggests
that the total number probably lies between 5 and 7 billion
copies." There are a lot of great books in the world, but
nothing tops God's Word! And it holds the answers to
cure all your worries! The more you learn about the Bible
and spend time reading it, the closer you get to God, the
more you grow as a follower of Jesus, and the more you
develop your prayer life too. So don't ever stop digging
into your Bible! It is your light to follow for your entire life.

*Dear God, thank You for giving us Your Word, the
Bible. Please guide me with it all my life. Amen.*

CRAVE GOD'S WORD

*I have looked for You with all my heart. Do not
let me turn from Your Law. Your Word have I hid
in my heart, that I may not sin against You.*
PSALM 119:10–11 NLV

The Bible is not a book that promises to keep you feeling
good or entertained. But it's not your typical book. It's a
living and active book from God Himself (Hebrews 4:12),
and it's His main way of speaking into your life and guiding
and correcting you.

It can be super hard to keep up good habits of reading
God's Word, especially with all the other things going on
in our lives. And we have a sin nature that tries to keep
us out of good habits and into bad ones. Plus, we have an
enemy, Satan, who fights for our attention and wants to
keep it on the world and meaningless things instead of
on God and the truth He wants us to hear. So, ask God
to help you look forward to spending time in His Word
every day. Ask Him to help you crave it.

*Dear God, I want to crave Your Word
and a relationship with You more than
anything else. Please help me. Amen.*

14

PAINFUL BUT GOOD

*God's Word is living and powerful. It is sharper than
a sword that cuts both ways. It cuts straight into
where the soul and spirit meet and it divides them.
It cuts into the joints and bones. It tells what the
heart is thinking about and what it wants to do.*
HEBREWS 4:12 NLV

This scripture about God's Word sounds painful. . .but that
doesn't mean it's bad for you. Think of other things that
are painful but good for you—like getting a good workout in sports or dance, which can be painful to muscles
but good and healthy in the long run as you strengthen
your body and build skill and endurance.

God's Word *can* be painful, but it is *always* so good for
you. It's painful when it's telling you what you're doing
wrong and how you need to change. But if you follow
it, you will be much healthier in the long run. As you're
growing in prayer, ask God to help you not to be afraid
of the good pain the Bible causes when it's helping you
get rid of sin in your life. Then let God fill up those places
with His goodness and love.

*Dear God, please let Your Word correct me
and teach me and make me healthy as I grow
closer to You and obey You. Amen.*

DON'T GIVE UP ON PRAYER

One day Jesus told his disciples a story to show that they should always pray and never give up. "There was a judge in a certain city," he said, "who neither feared God nor cared about people. A widow of that city came to him repeatedly, saying, 'Give me justice in this dispute with my enemy.' The judge ignored her for a while, but finally he said to himself, 'I don't fear God or care about people, but this woman is driving me crazy. I'm going to see that she gets justice, because she is wearing me out with her constant requests!' " Then the Lord said, "Learn a lesson from this unjust judge. Even he rendered a just decision in the end. So don't you think God will surely give justice to his chosen people who cry out to him day and night?"

LUKE 18:1–7 NLT

Jesus told this story to teach us to never give up on prayer. The point is that if a judge in the courts, who did not even respect God, was finally willing to help the woman who kept asking and asking, how much more will God help the people He loves who keep asking for His help?

Dear God, thank You that You want me to pray to You all the time. Help me to never give up on prayer. Amen.

PRAYER FOR YOUR PARENTS

"Honor your father and your mother, so your life may be long in the land the Lord your God gives you."

EXODUS 20:12 NLV

Maybe some of your worries come from family relationships. How are things going with your parents? It's a big job to be a mom or a dad, so I hope you're praying for your parents and working on having a good relationship with them as best you can. Good parents do so much to take good care of you. You're not always going to get along perfectly with them, but God's Word teaches you to honor them. In what ways do you feel stressed in your relationship with your parents? In what ways is it hardest to honor them? In what ways is it easiest?

Dear God, I need Your help to have great relationships with my parents. I want to do my best to honor my parents plus regularly pray for them. Help us to understand each other, love each other, and not stress each other out. Amen.

PRAYER FOR THE WHOLE FAMILY

But those who won't care for their relatives, especially those in their own household, have denied the true faith. Such people are worse than unbelievers.

1 TIMOTHY 5:8 NLT

We need to look out for one another in our families, especially the ones in our household, like our parents and siblings—but also our extended family, including grand-parents, aunts, uncles, and cousins. You might wonder what you can do to help take care of others in your family—and maybe that causes you worry. But it doesn't have to. With God's help, you can always offer encouragement and prayer for their needs. You can share God's love. And if there is conflict, you can try to help resolve it and be forgiving of others. God placed you in your family. Thank Him for each person, and ask Him to help you be a loving member of your family.

Dear God, I love my family, and I know You love them even more. Please help us to have good relationships. And please help any family members who don't believe in You to have a change of heart. Show me what I can do to share Your truth with them. Amen.

HOW TO PRAY

"Pray like this. . ."
MATTHEW 6:9 NLT

In the Bible, Jesus gave a specific example of how to pray that you've probably heard of—it's called the Lord's Prayer. In Matthew 6:9–13 (NLT), Jesus says, "Pray like this: Our Father in heaven, may your name be kept holy. May your Kingdom come soon. May your will be done on earth, as it is in heaven. Give us today the food we need, and forgive us our sins, as we have forgiven those who sin against us. And don't let us yield to temptation, but rescue us from the evil one."

This example from Jesus doesn't mean it's the only prayer we should ever pray, repeated word for word. It means He gave us an example of prayer; and each time we pray, we can model it. In all our prayers, we should be sincere and know that God is perfectly holy. We should pray for God's kingdom to come and for His will to be done. We should ask for our daily needs and for forgiveness for ourselves and for us to be able to forgive others. We should ask for help not to sin, and we should praise God.

Dear Jesus, thank You for teaching us the best way to pray. Help me to model Your prayer every day. Amen.

HEARING BUT NOT LISTENING

For I cried out to him for help, praising him as I
spoke. If I had not confessed the sin in my heart,
the Lord would not have listened. But God did
listen! He paid attention to my prayer.
PSALM 66:17–19 NLT

Do you ever hear something but not *really* listen? Sometimes if you're sitting in school, you can hear the teacher talking but you're not actually paying attention to what she's saying. Or maybe you heard your parents give you instructions or reminders, but you didn't focus and follow through.

God always hears our prayers because He is omniscient—He knows and sees all. But sometimes He doesn't *seem* to pay attention to our prayers. Why is that? Sometimes it's because we are holding on to sin in our lives rather than admitting it to God and asking for His help to get rid of it. Because of Jesus, we can admit all our sins, ask forgiveness, and be free of them. When we do, God gives full attention to our prayers.

Dear God, thank You for providing Jesus to free
me from my sin. I admit and confess my sin to
You. Thank You for taking it away. Thank You
for paying attention to my prayers. Amen.

LET CREATION GIVE YOU PEACE

*"But ask the wild animals, and they will teach you.
Ask the birds of the heavens, and let them tell
you. Or speak to the earth, and let it teach you.
Let the fish of the sea make it known to you. Who
among all these does not know that the hand of
the Lord has done this? In His hand is the life of
every living thing and the breath of all men."*
JOB 12:7–10 NLV

Go outside and look at a giant tree that grew from a
tiny seed, or watch a magnificent sunset display brilliant
colors across the sky, or listen to a bird sing a song that
no other creature can sing—these all can help put your
heart and mind and prayers at ease and give you peace.
Remember that all of creation started from nothing, and
then God spoke. He created and designed our world; He
created and designed each plant and flower and creature;
He created and designed each person in His image; and
He created and designed a plan to save us and give us
perfect eternal life with Him.

*Dear God, thank You for encouraging me and
giving me peace through everything You have
made in Creation. Remind me every day of
Your perfect power and purpose. Amen.*

IF ANYONE WANTS TO BE PROUD

*If anyone wants to be proud, he should be
proud of what the Lord has done.*
2 Corinthians 10:17 nlv

Sometimes the root cause of our anxiety is pride. We worry
too much about needing to look like we never mess up and
don't make mistakes. Or that we need to look perfect and
have the latest styles in makeup and clothes. Or we feel
like we need to keep up and be the best or at least better
than those around us in our schoolwork and activities.
God's Word tells us many times that pride is a sin that
can get us into lots of trouble. So, if we're going to be
proud about anything, it needs to be pride in what God
does. He is the one we should point others to as perfect,
certainly not ourselves. No person is perfect, and when
we can be humble and honestly admit our mistakes and
weaknesses and ways we don't measure up, we can then
help others see the need for everyone to have faith in our
perfect Savior, Jesus Christ.

*Dear God, I want to be proud of You alone. Help
me to see how every good thing I ever do ultimately
comes from You! Help me to show others both my
need and their need for Jesus as Savior. Amen.*

WHEN YOU'RE REJECTED

The more we suffer for Christ, the more God will
shower us with his comfort through Christ.
2 CORINTHIANS 1:5 NLT

Rejection hurts. Maybe someone you thought was a good friend left you out and ended the friendship. Maybe you tried out for a school play, positive you'd get a great role, but you didn't get chosen for any part. Or maybe you applied to your dream college, sure of your acceptance, but you didn't get in. In painful, confusing times like these, pour out your heart in prayer to God. He wants to pull you close, comfort you, and remind you that Jesus knows exactly what it's like to feel rejected. When you share with Him in suffering, you are bonding with Him, and through it, He's developing your faith and your character. He's also storing up rewards for you in heaven. Keep trusting and loving our Savior, and keep praying—no matter what rejection and suffering you go through. He is good through it all, and He is working to make all things right!

Dear Jesus, when I feel rejected, remind me how You
were rejected too. But, in Your rejection and suffering,
God was working to save the world. Remind me that You
are working in ways I'm not aware of when I am rejected
and suffering too. Please comfort me and strengthen
my faith as You work behind the scenes! Amen.

WRITE AND REMEMBER

"I will remember the deeds of the LORD;
yes, I will remember your miracles of long ago.
I will consider all your works
and meditate on all your mighty deeds."
PSALM 77:11–12 NIV

A great way to deal with worry is to journal. Jotting down your thoughts and fears and struggles can help you call them out as you see them named on paper. Once you have created a list, cross them out and write God's truth over top of them. Look back and remember how He has helped you with problems you worried about in the past. Write out your conversations with God and your praises and thanks to Him. Keep lists of the things you are asking of Him. Record when you see exactly how God answered your prayer. When you put dates on each of your prayer journal entries, you have a wonderfully true historical memory book to look back on and see how God has worked—and is working—in your life.

Dear God, I would love to get in the habit of writing down my prayers to You and recording how You answer my prayers too. Would You help me do this? Amen.

CHOOSE CAREFULLY

Test everything and do not let good things
get away from you. Keep away from
everything that even looks like sin.
1 Thessalonians 5:21–22 nlv

There are so many options in movies, TV, music, social media, and entertainment these days. And all those things can be a huge source of anxiety and temptation to sin, if we're not careful. We need to pray for wisdom about what we watch, listen to, read, and participate in on the internet. We should strive to be able to say, like David did in Psalm 101:1–5 (nlt):

I will sing of your love and justice, Lord. I will praise you with songs. I will be careful to live a blameless life—when will you come to help me? I will lead a life of integrity in my own home. I will refuse to look at anything vile and vulgar.

Dear God, please help guide me as I make entertainment and social media choices. Sometimes the options seem out of control, and it's sure not a popular choice to be careful! But I love You, and I want to stay away from the things that cause me anxiety and from anything that causes me to sin and disappoint You. Amen.

YOU ARE A MASTERPIECE

*We are God's masterpiece. He has created
us anew in Christ Jesus, so we can do the
good things he planned for us long ago.*
EPHESIANS 2:10 NLT

This scripture is a good one to memorize. It serves as a great reminder to give you confidence and peace and hope. You are no accident. Your life has purpose and meaning that God planned long ago when He created you. So, pray like this:

*Dear God, thank You for creating me totally unique.
Even my fingerprints are unlike those of any other
person in the world. I believe You have good plans
for me and good works You want me to do; and I
believe my life will be best when I'm following those
plans and doing those works! Will You please show
and guide me every day? Please put desires in my
heart and mind that match the things You want me
to do. Please help my schoolwork and the activities I
choose to prepare me for those things too. Please open
doors of opportunity You want me to walk through
and close doors You don't want for me. I want to live
a life of serving You and following Your will for me. I
believe that is the most rewarding kind of life! Amen.*

JESUS IS THE BREAD OF LIFE

*Jesus replied, "I am the bread of life. Whoever
comes to me will never be hungry again.
Whoever believes in me will never be thirsty."*
JOHN 6:35 NLT

What modern convenience would be the hardest and
most stressful for you to live without? Indoor plumbing?
Electricity? Air-conditioning? Wi-Fi? We are very blessed
today, and it would be super hard to adjust to not having
some of the conveniences we take for granted! But our
most basic daily needs for life are food and water, right?
We couldn't survive long without them. So, does Jesus say
in John 6 that He expects us to believe in Him and never
eat food or drink water again? No! But Jesus does want
us to stop worrying and simply trust in Him as the one
who provides for all our needs. *He* is really our most basic
need for life because He is the giver of life—eternal life!

*Dear Jesus, thank You for being the giver of life!
I trust in You. You are everything I need. Amen.*

MANAGE YOUR TIME WELL

*So be careful how you live. Live as men who
are wise and not foolish. Make the best use
of your time. These are sinful days.*
EPHESIANS 5:15–16 NLV

When we don't manage our time wisely, we cause ourselves all kinds of stress. Have you ever experienced this? Maybe you put off a project that was due or procrastinated on studying for a big exam—and then found yourself cramming at the last minute. Nearly everyone has. It's super easy to get distracted or to be lazy about doing the good work God has for us to do. What are the things that tempt you away from doing what you need to be doing? Maybe time with friends, social media, music, and TV? Ask God to help you have good self-discipline with those things. Then ask Him to show you how to live carefully and wisely, making the best use of your time and using your gifts to glorify Him in all the things He has planned for you to do.

*Dear God, help me to manage my time wisely to
accomplish the things I need to and the good things
You created me for so I can bring glory to You! Amen.*

PRAY FOR OUR NATION AND LEADERS

*Pray for kings and all others who are in power
over us so we might live quiet God-like lives
in peace. It is good when you pray like this.
It pleases God Who is the One Who saves.*
1 Timothy 2:2–3 nlv

If you pay attention to news about our nation and current events with laws and government, you might have plenty of extra worries and fears. Politics can be such a sad mess. You might think there's not much you can do, but there is *always* something. You can pray, of course! Pray for the leaders of our nation, the president and vice president and their families and all elected officials in federal, state, and local government and their families too. Praying for so many people might seem overwhelming, but let the American flag be a reminder. Every time you see it, you can pray something like this:

*Dear God, please bless our nation according to Your
will and give us peace. Help our leaders want to
acknowledge and honor You. Please give them Your
wisdom to govern well. May each of them know You as
the one true God and Savior. Please protect our nation
and protect our freedom to worship You; and help us to
use that freedom to spread Your truth and love. Amen.*

PRAY FOR THE WORLD

"Be still, and know that I am God! I will be honored by every nation. I will be honored throughout the world."
PSALM 46:10 NLT

❀

You can pray specifically for each state in our nation. You could put a map of the USA on a wall in your room to use as a visual reminder to pray and then choose a different state and its leaders to pray for each day.

And don't just stop there. God loves everyone everywhere in the whole world, not just our nation. You could get a globe and start praying for every person in every country and for all nations to honor the one true God and to do His will according to His Word. Spending time praying *for* the world is far better use of time than worrying about what's going on *in* the world!

Dear God, You love all people of all nations, and You want them to honor You and trust Jesus as Savior. You want to give them eternal life. You are such a good and loving heavenly Father. Help me to remember to pray for all people everywhere! Amen.

WHAT KIND OF MAN IS THIS?

Then he got into the boat and his disciples followed him. Suddenly a furious storm came up on the lake, so that the waves swept over the boat. But Jesus was sleeping. The disciples went and woke him, saying, "Lord, save us! We're going to drown!" He replied, "You of little faith, why are you so afraid?" Then he got up and rebuked the winds and the waves, and it was completely calm. The men were amazed and asked, "What kind of man is this? Even the winds and the waves obey him!"
MATTHEW 8:23–27 NIV

It's not just little kids that get freaked out by storms. No matter your age, storms and natural disasters can be scary and worrisome sometimes. But in any storm or flood or earthquake, Jesus has total power to protect. He can stop a storm or natural disaster with just His words if He chooses to so, of course, He can keep you safe.

Dear Jesus, You are so powerful to be able to just speak and immediately stop the winds and the waves. I don't ever want to stop being amazed by You! Help me to have great faith and never be afraid! Amen.

GOOD COMMUNICATION

The eyes of the Lord watch over those who do right; his ears are open to their cries for help.

PSALM 34:15 NLT

❀

To have good communication with God through our prayers, we must keep ourselves away from what is sinful. If we've asked Jesus to be our Savior, then we are right with God because of His grace. But that doesn't mean we should purposefully choose to lie or cheat or do anything that goes against God's Word again and again.

Romans 5:20–6:2 (NLT) says, "God's law was given so that all people could see how sinful they were. But as people sinned more and more, God's wonderful grace became more abundant. So just as sin ruled over all people and brought them to death, now God's wonderful grace rules instead, giving us right standing with God and resulting in eternal life through Jesus Christ our Lord. Well then, should we keep on sinning so that God can show us more and more of his wonderful grace? Of course not!"

Dear God, I know that because Jesus is my Savior, You take away my sin. But even though I am saved, I don't want to purposefully go against Your Word. I love You and want to please You. Amen.

WORK OUT AND PRAY

Pray in the Spirit at all times and on every occasion. Stay alert and be persistent in your prayers for all believers everywhere.
EPHESIANS 6:18 NLT

Do you ever pray while you take a long walk or a nice run? Or during any type of exercise or workout? Exercise is such a great way to relieve anxiety, stress, and worries. And adding prayer time into your workout is even better!

As you sweat it out in whatever your favorite form of exercise is, focus your mind on praying for your needs and the needs of others you know and love. Ask God to let any anxiety pour out of you along with all that sweat!

Dear God, sometimes I get too busy and distracted with so many things in life, and I don't take time to pray or exercise. I know I need both of those things daily to help deal with stress and worries. Please help me to form both good physical habits and prayer habits. Amen.

PRAYER AMONG FRIENDS, PART 1

Encourage one another and build each other up, just as in fact you are doing.
1 THESSALONIANS 5:11 NIV

At every stage of life, but especially in your teen years, you need good friends who encourage you—specifically those who encourage you to love and obey God. The right kinds of friends are such a blessing. And when you have good close friends, sometimes their worries become your worries too. You love and care about what's going on in their lives, and that's a good thing. Just be careful not to take on extra worry and anxiety you were never meant to carry. Be the friend who is always reminding other friends to cling tight to Jesus and cast those cares upon Him. Spend even more time in prayer talking to God about problems than you do talking about them with your friends. Jesus wants to help you and your friends with absolutely everything!

Dear God, thank You for my dear friends. Help us to talk even more to You than we do with each other, about anything and everything, because You care about it all. Amen.

PRAYER AMONG FRIENDS, PART 2

Two are better than one, because they have good
pay for their work. For if one of them falls, the
other can help him up. But it is hard for the one
who falls when there is no one to lift him up.
ECCLESIASTES 4:9–10 NLV

If you don't already have friends who love and follow Jesus like you do, ask God to bring some into your life. He will, though it might take some time. Sometimes He wants us to grow closer to Him first through prayer and His Word before He blesses us with a new friend. If you're already blessed with good Christian friends, thank God and ask Him to keep growing your good friendships! They are iron sharpening iron as Proverbs 27:17 says, which means good friends keep helping each other be and do their best.

Dear God, thank You that You want to bless
us with wonderful friends! Amen.

PRAYER AMONG FRIENDS, PART 3

Don't fool yourselves. Bad friends will destroy you.
1 Corinthians 15:33 cev

Friendships are so important and such a blessing, but they can also be the source of all kinds of stress and anxiety if you find yourself in the middle of bad friendships. While the Bible encourages you to have good friends, it also warns against having bad friends, like 1 Corinthians 15:33 says. If you find yourself in some bad friendships with people who are pushing you far away from love and obedience to God, you will need courage to end those friendships. Trust that God will help you be brave if you ask Him and fully depend on Him. And then be ready, knowing that those friends might not like your choices. If they treat you badly, hold on to this truth: "God blesses you when people mock you and persecute you and lie about you and say all sorts of evil things against you because you are my followers. Be happy about it! Be very glad! For a great reward awaits you in heaven" (Matthew 5:11–12 nlt).

Dear God, please help me to be wise about friendships and to have courage to end friendships that keep me from growing closer to You. Amen.

FOR THE GOOD OF THOSE WHO LOVE HIM

*God causes everything to work together
for the good of those who love God and are
called according to his purpose for them.*
ROMANS 8:28 NLT

The Bible promises that God makes everything work together for the good of those who love Him. But sometimes it doesn't make sense! Like when you prayed to make it on the team but were told you weren't good enough. Or, worse, you prayed so much for healing from an illness for a loved one, but that loved one died. It's heartbreaking and confusing.

Just because we're disappointed and hurting and can't understand, that doesn't mean God has changed or His promises aren't true. We must choose to trust Him even more when we don't understand Him. We must trust that His thoughts and ways are much higher than ours (Isaiah 55:8–9) and that He is working in ways we won't always understand in this world. But He promises that someday we will understand, and so we keep praying to Him and believing Him and learning from Him.

*Dear God, when I'm hurting and confused,
please hold me extra close and show me
Your love in special ways. Amen.*

SIMPLE JOYS

Be happy in your hope. Do not give up when trouble comes. Do not let anything stop you from praying.
ROMANS 12:12 NLV

❀

What are some of your favorite simple things that bring you joy? Maybe sunshine and bright blue skies. Maybe seeing a rainbow or fun shapes in the clouds. Maybe playing with your dog or grabbing an ice cream cone with a friend. A lot of sad and stressful things happen in this life, but God doesn't want us to be defeated by them (Romans 12:21). He gives us little things to delight in to help us through those hard times. And ultimately our joy doesn't depend on the situation we're going through; it depends on whether we know Jesus as Savior. With Him as our source of joy, we never run out of it!

Dear God, all my hope is in You, and all my joy comes from You! Thank You for all the little joys of life until one day we have constant, perfect joy forever in heaven with You! Amen.

BE HAPPY WITH WHATEVER YOU HAVE

*I have learned to be happy with whatever I
have. I know how to get along with little and
how to live when I have much. . . . I can do all
things because Christ gives me the strength.*
PHILIPPIANS 4:11–13 NLV

In a world filled with so many cool things—plus the internet and social media that tell us all about it instantly—we often struggle to be content with the life we've been given. And this can cause so much unnecessary anxiety. It's easy to look at other people's stuff and want what they have and want to do what they do instead of, or in addition to, the good things we already have and do. We need to pray hard against envy and greed, and we need to remember how to be happy and content: we simply must remember that we can do all things through Christ who gives us strength. Because He helps us, we can be happy and endure when we have too little; and we can be happy and give thanks when we have plenty. Jesus gives us strength, no matter what, and trusting in Him is where real contentment comes from!

*Dear God, please help me to be content
with whatever You decide to bless me with
and to trust in Your strength. Amen.*

ABSOLUTELY EVERYTHING

Pray about everything.
PHILIPPIANS 4:6 NLT

❀

A lot of super-important stuff goes on in our lives, and a lot of little stuff happens too. Does the one true God of the whole universe really want to hear about *everything*? Yes! Absolutely everything. It seems hard to believe, but He really does!

Think about it in terms of relationship. You care about all the things going on in the lives of your close family and friends because you love them so much. And God loves you so much more than even your closest family member or friend, so He cares about *every single detail* of your life. Look up Luke 12:7 in your Bible. God even knows the number of hairs on your head! So, anything that is stressing you out, or anything that is exciting you, or anything that is scaring you. . .remember that He cares and wants to hear about it all—the good and the bad, no matter how big or small.

Dear God, help me not to worry that anything is too silly or unimportant to talk to You about. Thank You for loving me so much and caring about everything I care about! Amen.

SAFE IN GOD'S CARE

*God is our safe place and our strength. He is always
our help when we are in trouble. So we will not be
afraid, even if the earth is shaken and the mountains fall
into the center of the sea, and even if its waters go wild
with storm and the mountains shake with its action.*

PSALM 46:1–3 NLV

Memorize and recite this scripture during any type of
worry or fear. We are *always* safe when we are in God's
care. He is our strength and our help in times of trouble—
even the worst kind of trouble we can possibly imagine.

*Dear God, I have nothing to fear because You
keep me safe. Please help me to remember that
You are my safe place in any and every life event.
Thank You for Your strength and help. Amen.*

PRAY LIKE JOB, PART 1

There was a man in the land of Uz whose name was Job. That man was without blame. He was right and good, he feared God, and turned away from sin.

JOB 1:1 NLV

It's hard to even imagine the extent of the pain and sorrow and stress and anxiety that Job had to endure. Yet after losing so much, including his livestock, his servants, and all his children, "Job stood up and tore his clothing and cut the hair from his head. And he fell to the ground and worshiped. He said, 'Without clothing I was born from my mother, and without clothing I will return. The Lord gave and the Lord has taken away. Praise the name of the Lord.' In all this Job did not sin or blame God" (Job 1:20–22 NLV).

We can follow Job's example in this prayer, and no matter what God gives to us or takes away from our lives, no matter what stress and anxiety we are facing, we can trust and worship God through it all.

Dear God, help me to have faith and endurance like Job so that no matter what hard things I have to go through, I will choose to trust and praise You. Amen.

PRAY LIKE JOB, PART 2

*"So I hate the things that I have said. And I put dust
and ashes on myself to show how sorry I am."*
JOB 42:6 NLV

Later, Job was tested even more, and he did not continue
to praise God through it all. He was very angry with God
for a while. But in the end, after God reminded Job of
His greatness and goodness, Job cried out in repentance,
telling God how sorry he was. We need to learn from Job
that when we cry out to God with angry words, we should
stop and realize God's power and love and control over all
things, in ways we cannot understand. And we need to say
we are sorry for disrespecting Him. After Job repented,
God blessed him again with even more than he had been
blessed in the first place!

*Dear God, help me to learn from Job that
if I speak in anger to You, I need to say I'm
sorry and continue to trust in You. Amen.*

REAL JOY

*When your faith remains strong through many trials,
it will bring you much praise and glory and honor on
the day when Jesus Christ is revealed to the whole
world. You love him even though you have never seen
him. Though you do not see him now, you trust him; and
you rejoice with a glorious, inexpressible joy. The reward
for trusting him will be the salvation of your souls.*
1 PETER 1:7–9 NLT

The Bible talks a lot about real joy that comes from knowing God and trusting Jesus as Savior. If you're ever feeling
anxious and need some extra reminders about joy, read
and hold on to scripture like 1 Peter 1:7–9 and these others:

- "You will show me the way of life. Being with You is
  to be full of joy. In Your right hand there is happiness
  forever" (Psalm 16:11 NLV).

- "If you obey My teaching, you will live in My love. In
  this way, I have obeyed My Father's teaching and live
  in His love. I have told you these things so My joy may
  be in you and your joy may be full" (John 15:10–11 NLV).

*Dear God, please remind me regularly of
the many reasons I have to be full of joy—
most of all because of You! Amen.*

WHO CAN EVER BE AGAINST YOU?

*If God is for us, who can ever be against us? Since
he did not spare even his own Son but gave him up
for us all, won't he also give us everything else?*
ROMANS 8:31–32 NLT

If you have accepted Jesus as your Savior and are following
Him, God is with you and for you. And like Romans says, if
God is for you, who can possibly be against you? You have
nothing to be afraid of or worried about—no situation or
person or test at school or bully or illness or injury will
ever be greater than God working in you and helping you.
And you only need to call on Him in prayer and believe
in His love and ability to help you. Make it a regular part
of your prayer time to praise God and tell Him how great
He is. You will remind yourself of what awesome power
you have helping you in all things!

*You are awesome, God! You are good and
strong and able to do anything! You are
loving and kind and generous! You are
everything to me, and I praise You! Amen.*

BUILD STRONG FAITH

*But you, dear friends, must build each other up
in your most holy faith, pray in the power of the
Holy Spirit, and await the mercy of our Lord Jesus
Christ, who will bring you eternal life. In this way,
you will keep yourselves safe in God's love.*
JUDE 20–21 NLT

No building can stand for long unless it has a strong foundation. And our lives need a strong foundation of faith in the one true God, or we can easily be overwhelmed and destroyed by stress and anxiety. Prayer is a major source of strength and support as you build your life of faith and strong foundation as a follower of Jesus. Spending time in God's Word, learning at a Bible-teaching church, serving God by serving others, and having fellowship with other Christians are all major sources of strength and support too. How are you doing in all these things?

Dear God, I want to be built up strong in my faith in You. Help me to pray, learn, and serve You all my days! Amen.

START A CONVERSATION

Is anyone among you in trouble? Let them pray.
Is anyone happy? Let them sing songs of praise.
JAMES 5:13 NIV

Do you ever do a "High/Low" conversation starter with friends or family, telling them about the best and worst parts of your day? It's so good to share and connect with people who care about us. These kinds of conversation starters can also be great prayer starters to your heavenly Father. Invite God into every conversation, knowing He's constantly present with you anyway and loves to be welcomed into your daily life. Tell Him about the different events of the day and how they made you feel, then give any worries and fears and needs to Him and praise Him for all the good things. He cares about every high and every low you have, plus everything in between too, because He loves you so much.

Dear God, please help me to remember Your
constant presence with me. I welcome You into
every part of my life, into every conversation.
I love You and need You! Amen.

GOD WANTS ALL PEOPLE TO BE SAVED

*[God] wants all people to be saved from the
punishment of sin. He wants them to come to
know the truth. There is one God. There is one Man
standing between God and men. That Man is Christ
Jesus. He gave His life for all men so they could
go free and not be held by the power of sin.*
1 TIMOTHY 2:4–6 NLV

Maybe, at times, you feel worried for the people you love
who don't trust Jesus as their Savior. Let this scripture
ease your anxiety. God loves those people dearly, even
more than you do—and He wants them to be saved. You
cannot force them to admit their sin and believe in and
accept Jesus, but you can pray for them. You can ask
God exactly what He wants you to do to best share His
truth and love with them. Don't ever give up on prayer,
and take action as God leads you. Simply trust in God's
perfect, loving plans.

*Dear God, thank You for wanting to save everyone from
the punishment of sin. Please use me to share Your truth
and love with anyone who needs to know it. Amen.*

FIGHT WORRY WITH WORSHIP SONGS

Come, let us sing with joy to the Lord. Let us sing loud with joy to the rock Who saves us. Let us come before Him giving thanks. Let us make a sound of joy to Him with songs. For the Lord is a great God, and a great King above all gods. The deep places of the earth are in His hand. And the tops of the mountains belong to Him. The sea is His, for He made it. And His hands made the dry land. Come, let us bow down in worship. Let us get down on our knees before the Lord Who made us. For He is our God.
PSALM 95:1–7 NLV

Spending time singing worship songs to God is one of the very best ways to fight worry! Great songs with lyrics that praise God and share biblical truth put your mind in exactly the place it needs to be. Worship songs are so easy to memorize, and whether you're in a place where you can crank the volume up or you need to just silently sing in your head, no one can ever stop you from worshipping God anytime and anyplace!

Dear God, I want songs of praise to You to fill my mind all the time and push out all the worries! Amen.

FIGHT WORRY WITH SCRIPTURE

I will study your commandments
and reflect on your ways.
I will delight in your decrees
and not forget your word.
Be good to your servant,
that I may live and obey your word.
Open my eyes to see
the wonderful truths in your instructions.
PSALM 119:15–18 NLT

While worship songs are great to have stuck in your head to fight worry, the exact words of scripture are even better. And, of course, you can sing scripture as songs too. Ask God to help scripture stick in your mind when you hear it and read it. It's a prayer He loves to answer, and so often He'll bring to mind exactly what you need and at just the right moment. His Word is how God wants to guide you and teach you, and He is so happy when you listen and obey!

Dear God, as I read, listen to, and learn Your Word,
please make the scriptures stick permanently in my
mind. I never want to forget them! Please bring them
to my attention at exactly the right times that I need
them, especially when I feel worried and afraid. Amen.

DON'T COMPLAIN

Do everything without complaining and arguing.
PHILIPPIANS 2:14 NLT

Sometimes we add extra stress to our lives by complaining about all the things we need to do or the tasks we don't like rather than just getting busy getting them done! It's a struggle for everyone at times because it's so easy to complain instead of work hard with a good attitude. But God's Word says not to complain about anything! And complaining makes the job even worse to get done, and it might even take longer to accomplish if we choose a bad attitude while we work. So, focus hard on not complaining the next time you have an unpleasant job to do. Choose praise and prayer instead. Ask God to help you make a habit of pushing negativity and complaints out of your mind.

Dear God, help me not to add more stress to my life with negativity. I need Your help to replace complaining with good and positive thoughts, especially praise and worship to You! Amen.

GOOD COMMUNICATION

"If your brother sins against you, go and tell him what he did without other people hearing it."
MATTHEW 18:15 NLV

Complaining should never be confused with communicating and working through conflict. We need to have hard conversations sometimes to help improve relationships and situations, especially the ones causing us lots of stress—those need to be resolved ASAP! Maybe you've dealt with this kind of thing. For example, telling a friend you're frustrated with the unfair way she's been treating you is *not* complaining. You need to talk and work out the situation together. We should pray for God to help us embrace good communication and healthy conflict. Fear of healthy conflict is one of Satan's tactics that lets people keep sinning against others rather than working toward good relationships and teamwork.

Dear God, help me to be wise and know the difference between complaining and good communication. I want to be able to work out conflict with people in my life in good and healthy ways with Your help! Amen.

GOD'S REAL LOVE

And now these three remain: faith, hope and
love. But the greatest of these is love.
1 CORINTHIANS 13:13 NIV

Our world has a lot of wrong ideas about what love is, and that causes a lot of anxiety, even if many people won't admit it. God *is* love, 1 John 4:8 tells us. All real love flows from Him and His Word. None of us would know anything about love if not for God! So, we need *His* instructions about love more than anything else. First Corinthians 13:4–8 (NIV) teaches us that real love "is patient, love is kind. It does not envy, it does not boast, it is not proud. It does not dishonor others, it is not self-seeking, it is not easily angered, it keeps no record of wrongs. Love does not delight in evil but rejoices with the truth. It always protects, always trusts, always hopes, always per-severes. Love never fails."

Dear God, help me to learn and live by what You say
about real love—because You are real love! Amen.

BE STILL, PART 1

"Be still, and know that I am God."
PSALM 46:10 ESV

Our phones are so fantastic with all the things they can do and ways they can help us stay in touch. They can be really distracting too. Have you ever tried to talk with someone who kept checking their phone for new texts or updates? It's rude, isn't it? A good conversation with a good friend is a focused conversation that shows each other you care and truly want to listen to each other. Prayer to God needs to be the same way—even better, actually! God knows and understands we have distractions in this life, but we need to work hard to put all distractions out of our minds when we pray and realize exactly who we're talking to in prayer. We should go to God with respect and total devotion because He is the King of all kings who loves us and lets us come to Him at any and all times—*amazing!*

Dear God, help me to be still and respectful before You—with my thoughts and conversation completely focused on and devoted to You! Amen.

BE STILL, PART 2

Be still before the LORD and wait patiently for him;
fret not yourself over the one who prospers in his
way, over the man who carries out evil devices!
PSALM 37:7 ESV

When you pray, "be still" like scripture says. Be patient without fretting. Steady your mind and heart, and concentrate on who God is and how much praise He deserves. Tell Him how you love and adore Him. Ask forgiveness for your sins. Thank Him for being your Savior. And then tell Him all your needs and your loved ones' needs. He loves to hear and help with it all.

Dear God, You are King of kings and Lord of lords.
You are Almighty Creator. You are my Savior from
sin. You are all this and more, and You are my loving
heavenly Father as well. I am beyond blessed to
be able to come to You in prayer. You know my
thoughts and needs and worries, and You care about
each and every one. I bring them to You today,
and I ask for Your help and Your peace. Amen.

AS ONE SPEAKS TO A FRIEND

*Inside the Tent of Meeting, the Lord would speak
to Moses face to face, as one speaks to a friend.*
EXODUS 33:11 NLT

❀

There is so much to learn from Moses' life as recorded in the Bible. He was very close to God and would even speak with Him face-to-face like you'd speak to a friend! Yet later in Exodus 33, we learn that Moses could not look directly at God's face because His glory was just too great! Reading this passage reminds us how awesome our God is and how He wants to be in close relationship with His people.

We can humbly ask to have great favor with God while we respect and follow His Word. Pray like Moses: "If it is true that you look favorably on me, let me know your ways so I may understand you more fully and continue to enjoy your favor" (Exodus 33:13 NLT).

*Dear God, I want to make You happy and have Your
favor on me. I humbly ask You to delight in me as
I obey You. Please help me to grow in Your ways
and understand You more every day. Amen.*

AVOIDING DRAMA

*"Blessed are the peacemakers, for they
will be called children of God."*

Matthew 5:9 niv

Some people seem to love drama just for the sake of drama. If some sort of drama isn't happening, they'll surely create it. We shouldn't love being in conflict and competition with others; instead, we should always want good and peaceful relationships, forgiving each other and not gossiping or causing fights.

Yet the Bible says blessed are the peace*makers*, and you can't *make* anything without some work involved. So, it takes some working through of disagreements and trouble to make peace sometimes—not just going along with anything to try to keep everyone happy and drama-free. We need a lot of help and wisdom from God to know how to do this right. Fortunately, God promises us that He loves to give us wisdom (see James 1:5). He loves to help us with our problems, so just keep asking!

*Dear God, help me to avoid drama yet also be
someone willing to work out conflict and be a
peacemaker. I am so grateful for Your wisdom
and help. I need You so much! Amen.*

PLEASE GOD, NOT OTHER PEOPLE

I'm not trying to win the approval of people,
but of God. If pleasing people were my
goal, I would not be Christ's servant.
GALATIANS 1:10 NLT

We often worry far too much about getting the approval of others. To want approval means you want to be accepted and liked. And it's hard not to want that when you desire to have friends and get along well with people. But God's Word shows us we shouldn't be looking for approval from people. We should look for God's approval most of all. If you start praying now to be a God pleaser and a servant of Jesus—not a people pleaser—you'll benefit in so many ways! You won't be so worried what other people think of you. You won't want to give in to peer pressure. You'll be true to the unique, amazing person God designed you to be and follow the good plans He has for you. Yes, living for God's approval instead of people's can be hard! But as you pray, God will help you keep your focus on Him; and at the same time, He'll be filling your life with the good and loving relationships you need with others.

Dear God, I love You most and want to please
You, not other people. It's a struggle, though.
I'm trusting You will help me. Amen.

GO WITH TRUST TO THE THRONE OF GOD

*[Jesus] understands our weaknesses, for he faced
all of the same testings we do, yet he did not sin.
So let us come boldly to the throne of our gracious
God. There we will receive his mercy, and we will
find grace to help us when we need it most.*
HEBREWS 4:15–16 NLT

No matter what worries you or makes you feel nervous
and "less than" in this world, because of Jesus, you never
need to feel intimidated about going to the royal throne
of almighty God! The Bible says we can approach Him
with complete trust and ask for His help whenever we
need it, and He will give His love and kindness and favor
every time! Knowing that truth, you never need to feel
intimidated about anything. God is with you and is helping
you, no matter what you face! The King of kings wants you
to ask for His help—with everything. Amazing!

*Dear God, thank You that You allow me to ask
You for help with anything and everything.
Never let me forget that! Amen.*

PRAY WITH THE RIGHT ATTITUDE

"Two men went to the Temple to pray. One was a Pharisee, and the other was a despised tax collector. The Pharisee stood by himself and prayed this prayer: 'I thank you, God, that I am not like other people—cheaters, sinners, adulterers. I'm certainly not like that tax collector! I fast twice a week, and I give you a tenth of my income.' But the tax collector stood at a distance and dared not even lift his eyes to heaven as he prayed. Instead, he beat his chest in sorrow, saying, 'O God, be merciful to me, for I am a sinner.' I tell you, this sinner, not the Pharisee, returned home justified before God. For those who exalt themselves will be humbled, and those who humble themselves will be exalted."

Luke 18:10–14 NLT

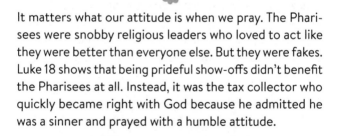

It matters what our attitude is when we pray. The Pharisees were snobby religious leaders who loved to act like they were better than everyone else. But they were fakes. Luke 18 shows that being prideful show-offs didn't benefit the Pharisees at all. Instead, it was the tax collector who quickly became right with God because he admitted he was a sinner and prayed with a humble attitude.

Dear God, I want to come to You honestly and humbly about who I am, what I've done, and what I need. Amen.

REAL STRONG WOMEN

*If Christ keeps giving me his power, I will gladly brag
about how weak I am. Yes, I am glad to be weak or
insulted or mistreated or to have troubles and sufferings,
if it is for Christ. Because when I am weak, I am strong.*
2 CORINTHIANS 12:9–10 CEV

Sometimes the world's idea of strong women is very different from God's will and His ways. To be truly strong,
pray for God to help you be strong *in Him*. The Bible tells
us to be happy about our weaknesses because when we
can admit we are weak, we can ask God for His power
and He will keep giving it! On our own, we could never
have greater power than God's, so being filled with God's
limitless power is absolutely amazing! He loves to give His
strength, so look at your weakness as a blessing, admit it,
and then ask God to make you a mighty young woman in
His power and according to His perfect plans!

*Dear God, I admit my many weaknesses. I'm glad for
them because they make me depend on You. Please fill
me with Your awesome power and strength, and make
me a truly strong young woman. Thank You! Amen.*

FAR MORE THAN YOU COULD IMAGINE

God can do anything, you know—far more than you could ever imagine or guess or request in your wildest dreams! He does it not by pushing us around but by working within us, his Spirit deeply and gently within us.
EPHESIANS 3:20–21 MSG

Have you ever received a whole lot more than what you had hoped or asked for your birthday or Christmas? Or maybe you were working hard to do well on a test at school, and when the graded test came back, you realized you did even better than what you expected. So exciting!

Every time you pray, think about how God can do far more than anything you can dream up! Remember that He doesn't always work in the ways you want or expect, but His plans are *always* better, and He is so trustworthy. He loves you and wants what is best for you in every single situation.

Dear God, I want to pray to You in big ways. Then I want to remember that You can do far more than anything my imagination can dream up. I believe You love me and will do what's best for me all the time. Amen.

DON'T FORGET TO BE GRATEFUL

*Ten men with a bad skin disease came to Him. They
stood a little way off. They called to Him, "Jesus!
Teacher! Take pity on us!" When Jesus saw them,
He said, "Go and show yourselves to the religious
leaders." As they went, they were healed. One of them
turned back when he saw he was healed. He thanked
God with a loud voice. . . . Jesus asked, "Were there
not ten men who were healed? Where are the other
nine? Is this stranger from another country the only
one who turned back to give thanks to God?"*

LUKE 17:12–18 NLV

Focusing on gratitude is a great way to soothe anxiety.
But sometimes we just forget to be grateful. This account
in Luke 17 reminds us how easy it is to forget to say thank
you. Jesus had just miraculously healed these ten men.
You'd think they would have been bursting with thanks.
Yet only one of them turned back to Jesus to actually
thank and worship Him. In whatever ways God blesses
us, we should always want to be like the one man and not
the other nine!

*Dear God, please help me not to forget to be
grateful. You are so good to me, and I have so
many blessings to focus on. I want to worship and
praise and thank You for everything. Amen.*

RENEW YOUR MIND

Take hold of every thought and make it obey Christ.
2 CORINTHIANS 10:5 NLV

Because we live in a world full of unbelievers, sometimes we spend too much time studying what they do and say and think—especially through the internet and social media—and soon that seems to be all that's filling our minds. We even start to copy them and go along with trends that go against God's Word. If that's happening, we need a renewal of our minds, and God is the one to renew it! His Word says, "Do not act like the sinful people of the world. Let God change your life. First of all, let Him give you a new mind. Then you will know what God wants you to do. And the things you do will be good and pleasing and perfect" (Romans 12:2 NLV).

Dear God, when my mind is filling up with the things of this world, please renew my mind. Refocus it on You and what You want for my life! Amen.

KEEP WATCH AND PRAY

*"Keep watch and pray, so that you will
not give in to temptation. For the spirit
is willing, but the body is weak!"*
MATTHEW 26:41 NLT

Do you ever plan to study hard and ahead of time for an upcoming test but then find yourself quickly cramming the night before? Do you ever plan to have regular quiet time with God and His Word, but you keep letting the busyness of the day get in the way? Sometimes we have the very best plans to do a good job with something, and then we just don't follow through. We are human, and we have struggles and temptations that keep us from doing good. That's why we need to pray for God to help us. We need to tell Him, "I can't do this on my own! Because of sin, I'm tempted to mess up all the time! I need Your great big power working in me to overcome this temptation."

*Dear God, I sure do need Your great big power
working in me to help with my struggles and
temptations. I can't do anything good without
You! Please help me with everything! Amen.*

WHEN EVERYTHING SEEMED HOPELESS

"Now, O Lord our God, I beg You to save us."
2 KINGS 19:19 NLV

If your worries and stresses are completely overwhelming you, especially if enemies are the cause, learn from Hezekiah, the king of Judah, who prayed when the cities of Judah were captured by enemies and everything seemed hopeless:

"O LORD, God of Israel. . .You alone are God of all the kingdoms of the earth. You alone created the heavens and the earth. Bend down, O LORD, and listen! Open your eyes, O LORD, and see! . . . It is true, LORD, that the kings of Assyria have destroyed all these nations. And they have thrown the gods of these nations into the fire and burned them. But of course the Assyrians could destroy them! They were not gods at all—only idols of wood and stone shaped by human hands. Now, O LORD our God, rescue us from his power; then all the kingdoms of the earth will know that you alone, O LORD, are God" (2 Kings 19:15–19 NLT).

God answered Hezekiah's prayer and rescued Judah from the evil Assyrians. Let Hezekiah's prayer inspire you to pray like this:

Dear God, when everything seems hopeless and I feel like I have enemies controlling me, please come to my rescue like You did for Hezekiah. I know You can! Amen.

LIKE YOUR CREATOR

The LORD is the everlasting God,
the Creator of all the earth.
ISAIAH 40:28 NLT

❀

Have you ever been so worried over a project for school in which you needed to be super creative, but you just felt totally stuck and unable? In those stressful times, remember *whose* you are! You are a child of the almighty Creator God. Remember that after God put earth, sky, water, sun, moon, and stars in place, He created every cool plant and animal and then people. Genesis 1:27 (NLT) says, "God created human beings in his own image. In the image of God he created them; male and female he created them." Never forget that you are made in His image! So, ask Him to help you with some fresh new ideas and then keep thinking and working. You might be surprised how He answers with new ideas popping into your brain!

Dear God, You designed me with a brain that is
capable of so much. Help me to use it well and
to think and do like You want me to. I want to be
creative like You, my amazing Creator! Amen.

WITH NO DOUBTS

*I write this letter to you who believe in the Son of God.
I write so that you will know that you have eternal life
now. We can come to God with no doubts. This means
that when we ask God for things (and those things agree
with what God wants for us), then God cares about what
we say. God listens to us every time we ask him. So we
know that he gives us the things that we ask from him.*
1 JOHN 5:13–15 ICB

Our doubts are a huge cause of our worries at times!
But when we believe in Jesus Christ, we have eternal life
and can pray to God with no doubts! And when we ask
Him for things that agree with what He wants for us, He
cares, He listens, and He gives us what we ask for. So how
do we know what He wants for us so that we can pray in
agreement? We read His Word and pray to Him and keep
drawing closer to Him every day of our lives! As we draw
near to Him, He draws near to us.

*Dear God, I want to spend more and more time
with You and continue to learn more about
what You want for me. Help my prayers match
Your purpose and Your plans for me! Amen.*

DON'T WORRY ABOUT WEALTH

We brought nothing into the world, and we can take nothing out of it. But if we have food and clothing, we will be content with that. Those who want to get rich fall into temptation and a trap and into many foolish and harmful desires that plunge people into ruin and destruction. For the love of money is a root of all kinds of evil. Some people, eager for money, have wandered from the faith and pierced themselves with many griefs.
1 Timothy 6:7–10 niv

A lot of people make their life goals based on what will help them gain more money, and what they're really setting themselves up for is a life full of anxiety. Choose now, while you are young, not to make wealth your focus. Instead, trust God's Word when it says that getting trapped in pursuing lots of money can lead to all kinds of sin and foolish things. Let God help you focus on goals that match His good plans for your life.

Dear God, please help me never to worry about wealth. I don't want my life goals to be about money; I want them to be about serving You and doing the good things You have planned for me! Amen.

PROBLEMS AND TRIALS

We can rejoice, too, when we run into problems and trials, for we know that they help us develop endurance. And endurance develops strength of character, and character strengthens our confident hope of salvation. And this hope will not lead to disappointment. For we know how dearly God loves us, because he has given us the Holy Spirit to fill our hearts with his love.

ROMANS 5:3–5 NLT

It's so easy to hate the problems and trials we face that cause us so much worry. But we need to remember that when we depend on Jesus to help us get through them, our problems are also doing good things for us—they are helping us develop endurance. And like this scripture says, that helps us develop strong character, which then strengthens our confident hope of salvation in Jesus! God's Word promises that our hope in Him will never disappoint us. So, as hard as the problems and trials are, don't forget about the good things they can do for you as well. Stick close to Jesus in prayer, spend time in God's Word, and let Him love you and lead you.

Dear God, help me to rejoice in problems and suffering. It's so hard sometimes, but You want me to learn to depend on You through them— and that kind of dependence is such a blessing! Thank You for loving me so well. Amen.

BEAUTY FROM THE INSIDE

*Your beauty should come from the inside. It should
come from the heart. This is the kind that lasts.*
1 PETER 3:4 NLV

Measuring up to the latest fashion trends can cause you anxiety—but only if you let it. Does real beauty and a person's value come from outer appearance? Definitely not. You might know people who wear the best clothes and always look super cool, but they're snobby and mean. And maybe you know people who never have the best clothes and who don't ever follow the latest trends in hair and makeup, but they have kindness and honesty and love overflowing out of them for others. So don't let keeping up with trends cause you any worries. God focuses on the heart of people, not the outward appearance, and you can too—for both yourself and others.

*Dear God, help me not to worry about outward
appearances. I want to be known for real and
lasting beauty that comes from my heart, because
I truly love You and love others. Amen.*

BE INSPIRED BY ANNA

*Anna, a prophet, was also there in the Temple. She was
the daughter of Phanuel from the tribe of Asher, and
she was very old. Her husband died when they had been
married only seven years. Then she lived as a widow
to the age of eighty-four. She never left the Temple
but stayed there day and night, worshiping God with
fasting and prayer. She came along just as Simeon was
talking with Mary and Joseph, and she began praising
God. She talked about the child to everyone who had
been waiting expectantly for God to rescue Jerusalem.*

LUKE 2:36–38 NLT

Anna was a woman of Bible times who still inspires us today.
She had lost her husband after they'd been married only
seven years, and that had to be so sad and stressful. Yet
she wanted to serve God wholeheartedly and pray all the
time. She was delighted when Jesus was born and praised
God because she knew Jesus was our Savior.

*Dear God, help me to be like Anna, serving You
no matter what and wanting to pray more and
more so I can grow ever closer to You. Amen.*

GOD WILL COME NEAR

Come near to God and he will come near to you.
JAMES 4:8 NIV

Sometimes when you're stressed and worried and trying to pray, God might feel far away. But could that have anything to do with what your relationship with God has looked like lately? Each one of us must put time and effort into our relationship with Jesus. He is the Savior of everyone who believes in Him, but He doesn't want to be a distant Savior we meet once and never hang out with again. He wants to be the closest kind of friend, and He is constantly with us through His Holy Spirit! We grow closer to Jesus by regularly spending time reading the Bible, going to a Bible-teaching church, serving others in Jesus' name, and praying to Him all the time.

Dear God, I want You as my true closest friend!
Thank You for always being there for me! Amen.

GO TO CHURCH

Let us help each other to love others and to do good. Let us not stay away from church meetings.
HEBREWS 10:24–25 NLV

You'll grow in your relationship with Jesus and in your prayer life by regularly going to church. We often think of church as just a building we go to, when really the Church is a group of people—all followers of Jesus Christ, all around the world. But since we can't all meet in the same place at once, we do have buildings all over the place where we can meet together. We always need to keep learning more about God and His Word, and we need time with other people who love and want to worship God. It's so good to be together, to comfort and encourage each other, to learn together and sing and pray to God together. There are so many types and styles of churches, but the most important thing about any of them is that they must preach the whole Word of God and do what it says—and glorify God by doing so.

Dear God, thank You for Your Church. Help me to be active in it my whole life. Amen.

SERVE

" 'For I was hungry, and you fed me. I was thirsty, and
you gave me a drink.' . . . "Then these righteous ones
will reply, 'Lord, when did we ever see you hungry
and feed you? Or thirsty and give you something
to drink?' . . . "And the King will say, 'I tell you the
truth, when you did it to one of the least of these my
brothers and sisters, you were doing it to me!' "
MATTHEW 25:35, 37, 40 NLT

Reading God's Word in daily devotion time, praying constantly, worshipping God, and learning at church are all
ways we grow in our relationship with Jesus. And these
verses from Matthew 25 show us exactly how to be extra
close to Jesus. We serve Him directly when we feed the
hungry, give water to the thirsty, share clothes with the
needy, and so on. Let yourself grow closer to Jesus by
serving others in need. And when you serve others in
need, it often helps get your mind off your own worries
and fills you with gratitude for what you have. Pray for God
to show you many opportunities for service all your life!

Dear God, I want to serve You and draw
close to You by serving others. Show me
who, where, when, and how. Amen.

SHADRACH, MESHACH, AND ABEDNEGO

Furious with rage, Nebuchadnezzar summoned Shadrach, Meshach and Abednego.

DANIEL 3:13 NIV

Shadrach, Meshach, and Abednego were about to be thrown into a fire so hot no one could even get near it without dying, but they refused to give up their faith in the one true God to worship a false god. God gave them such courage that they were able to say to King Nebuchadnezzar, "If we are thrown into the fire, our God Whom we serve is able to save us from it. And He will save us from your hand, O king. But even if He does not, we want you to know, O king, that we will not serve your gods or worship the object of gold that you have set up" (Daniel 3:17–18 NLV).

"Even if He does not," they said. It's not that they didn't believe God had the power to save them. But they trusted that God's will is always best, no matter what He decides.

Dear God, please help me to have brave trust and always be able to say that even if You choose not to answer my prayer, I will never stop believing in You! You are always good and always right! Amen.

MORNING PRAYERS

*In the morning, Lord, you hear my
voice; in the morning I lay my requests
before you and wait expectantly.*
PSALM 5:3 NIV

Are you a night owl or an early bird? Do you wake up
eager and ready to go, or are you dragging your feet?
Whatever the case, do your best to start your day with
prayer. Even before you get out of bed, ask God how
you can best serve Him today. Ask Him to bless you and
keep you close to Him. Ask Him to help you depend on
His strength and power. Ask Him to give you wisdom and
teach you and guide you. And ask Him to help you share
His love and truth with others.

*Dear God, please help my thoughts first go to You when
I wake up! Show me how to serve You each day. Please
bless me and help me to stay close to You. Please give
me Your strength and power through Your Holy Spirit.
Please give me wisdom. Teach me and guide me to share
Your truth and love with those around me. Amen.*

BE WILLING TO LET GO

*I focus on this one thing: Forgetting the past and
looking forward to what lies ahead, I press on to reach
the end of the race and receive the heavenly prize
for which God, through Christ Jesus, is calling us.*
PHILIPPIANS 3:13–14 NLT

We often worry too much about letting go. When it's
time for something new in our lives, we don't want to
give up the old. Or sometimes we don't want to share
what we have with others because we're afraid then
we won't have enough. But there's a popular saying
that we can't accept new gifts from God if we keep
a tight fist clutching what we already have. An open
hand that is willing to let go when we need to is a hand
that can receive new gifts.

*Dear God, please loosen my fists from the gifts You
give me. Help me to know when I need to let go and be
generous and willing to experience new things You are
doing in my life and new gifts You are giving. Amen.*

BE HUMBLE: ASK FOR THE RIGHT REASONS

"If my people, who are called by my name, will humble themselves and pray and seek my face and turn from their wicked ways, then I will hear from heaven, and I will forgive their sin and will heal their land."

2 CHRONICLES 7:14 NIV

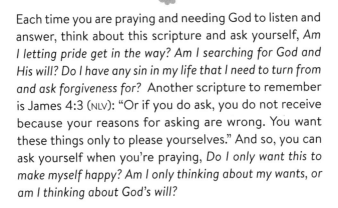

Each time you are praying and needing God to listen and answer, think about this scripture and ask yourself, *Am I letting pride get in the way? Am I searching for God and His will? Do I have any sin in my life that I need to turn from and ask forgiveness for?* Another scripture to remember is James 4:3 (NLV): "Or if you do ask, you do not receive because your reasons for asking are wrong. You want these things only to please yourselves." And so, you can ask yourself when you're praying, *Do I only want this to make myself happy? Am I only thinking about my wants, or am I thinking about God's will?*

Dear God, help me to be humble and ask You for things with the right motives. I want to look for You more than I look for anything for myself. Please help me. Amen.

PRAYER IN SCHOOL

The fear of the LORD is the beginning of knowledge,
but fools despise wisdom and instruction.
PROVERBS 1:7 NIV

A lot of your worries might have to do with what's going on at school. There you have a lot of opportunities to learn, and you have a lot of opportunities to pray too! Any believer can pray silently, at any time, for God to help in any school situation. You can pray for all the teachers and staff. You can pray for your classmates. You can pray for opportunities to share God's love. You can pray for God to help you focus and do your best on tests and projects. You can pray for good relationships with classmates and teachers. You can pray for peace and safety at your school. And on and on! No one can ever stop you from silent prayer. Make your school and everything about it a big priority in your prayers, and then watch how God works!

Dear God, I need Your help at school every day in a zillion ways, and so does everyone at school. Thank You for caring about each and every concern I have. Amen.

YOUR GOOD SHEPHERD

The Lord is my Shepherd.
PSALM 23:1 NLV

Focus on the comfort and peace of Psalm 23 as you pray. God is your loving Shepherd, but if you're not following Him, where will you end up? If you do let Him lead and guide you, you will find everything you need, plus peace and joy in any situation.

Psalm 23 continues:

I will have everything I need. He lets me rest in fields of green grass. He leads me beside the quiet waters. He makes me strong again. He leads me in the way of living right with Himself which brings honor to His name. Yes, even if I walk through the valley of the shadow of death, I will not be afraid of anything, because You are with me. You have a walking stick with which to guide and one with which to help. These comfort me. You are making a table of food ready for me in front of those who hate me. You have poured oil on my head. I have everything I need. For sure, You will give me goodness and loving-kindness all the days of my life. Then I will live with You in Your house forever. (Psalm 23:1–6 NLV)

Dear Lord, thank You for being my Shepherd and providing everything I need. Amen.

IDENTITY

And God made man in His own likeness. In the likeness of God He made him. He made both male and female.
GENESIS 1:27 NLV

You hear a lot about people trying to figure out their identity. If we look to God, that's where we find it! His Word is clear in Genesis 1 that God made people either male or female in His likeness. He has given us the Bible to guide us in how to live and love like He does. If you have accepted Jesus as your Savior, then celebrate the fact that you can say this: "Christ lives in me. The life I now live in this body, I live by putting my trust in the Son of God. He was the One Who loved me and gave Himself for me" (Galatians 2:20 NLV).

Dear God, please help me to always know that my identity is found in You! Thank You for creating me and saving me from sin! I live my life fully trusting in You and following Jesus Christ, who lives in me! Amen.

ENDURANCE

*We are pressed on every side by troubles, but
we are not crushed. We are perplexed, but not
driven to despair. We are hunted down, but never
abandoned by God. We get knocked down, but we
are not destroyed. Through suffering, our bodies
continue to share in the death of Jesus so that the
life of Jesus may also be seen in our bodies.*
2 CORINTHIANS 4:8–10 NLT

Think of a time when you've needed lots of endurance.
Maybe during a sport or activity like cross country or
dance. Or maybe during a really hard test at school when
you felt super stressed and wanted to give up but didn't.
The Bible talks about how we will sometimes have so
much trouble in our lives that it feels like we are almost
completely defeated. But God will always help us have
just enough new strength and energy to not give up. He
will hold us up and keep us going!

*Dear God, I trust that You will keep giving
me more strength, energy, and endurance
just when I feel like giving up. I will never be
defeated when You are helping me! Amen.*

REMEMBER TO PRAY FOR YOUR LEADERS OF FAITH

Remember your leaders who taught you the word of God. Think of all the good that has come from their lives, and follow the example of their faith.
HEBREWS 13:7 NLT

If you keep a prayer journal, it's a great idea to list all the people who have helped you in the past and are still helping to lead you in your faith. Thank God for these specific people and how they encouraged and taught you to know God and follow Jesus. Ask Him to bless them. If you know some of their specific needs, talk to God about those things. Mostly, pray for Christian leaders to continue to be strong in their faith, no matter what life brings their way, and to be leaders to others in addition to you!

Dear God, thank You for the awesome people You have put in my life who have helped me to know and love You. I am so grateful for them. Please bless and help them in everything. Help us to encourage each other as we live for You and lead others to You! Amen.

BE HAPPY ABOUT IT!

If you are insulted because you bear the
name of Christ, you will be blessed, for the
glorious Spirit of God rests upon you.
1 PETER 4:14 NLT

If you're insulted for being a Christian, don't let it get you down. Be happy about it! Maybe that sounds absurd, but God's Word tells us we should not be ashamed; we should be thankful instead. God's Spirit is in you, and you are saved forever, so don't worry about what anyone else might say to ridicule you. Matthew 5:11–12 (NLT) says, "God blesses you when people mock you and persecute you and lie about you and say all sorts of evil things against you because you are my followers. Be happy about it! Be very glad! For a great reward awaits you in heaven."

Dear Jesus, help me not to get upset if people insult
or ridicule me because I love and follow You. Give
me wisdom about what the Bible says. Remind
me to be happy because You have saved me and
my rewards will be great in heaven. Amen.

PRAY AND PROVIDE FOR
THOSE IN NEED

*Whoever is kind to the poor lends to the LORD, and
he will reward them for what they have done.*

PROVERBS 19:17 NIV

❀

You've probably encountered homeless and needy people
in various places. Maybe your heart aches and you worry
for these people. That shows your loving heart and the
Spirit of God in you caring for people. Only God fully
knows exactly how they got to this point and exactly what
they need. You can pray for God to give them the shelter
and provisions they need, and you can ask God what He
wants you to do to help. Talk to your parents about what
they would allow you to do and how you can help together
as a family. Maybe you'll want to put together blessing
bags full of snacks and water and a Bible plus hygiene items
to pass out when you see a needy person on the streets.
Maybe you can volunteer at a shelter or food pantry.
Find out what your church does to help the needy in your
community and join in! Always, you can keep asking God to
give you compassion and wisdom—and be ready to obey
as He leads you to care for people in need.

*Dear God, thank You for my many blessings. Help me
to share them with those who have so little. Amen.*

GOD CAN NEVER BE PRAISED ENOUGH

I lift you high in praise, my God, O my King!
and I'll bless your name into eternity.

PSALM 145:1 MSG

Sometimes God will answer prayer exactly like you hoped and prayed for. But no matter how God answers your prayers, He always deserves your gratitude and praise—so tell Him that. Thank Him with your words. Sing Him your favorite worship songs. Read and repeat beautiful psalms of the Bible to Him, like this one:

I lift you high in praise, my God, O my King!
and I'll bless your name into eternity.
I'll bless you every day,
and keep it up from now to eternity.
GOD is magnificent; he can never be praised enough.
There are no boundaries to his greatness.
Generation after generation stands in awe of your work;
each one tells stories of your mighty acts.
Your beauty and splendor have everyone talking;
I compose songs on your wonders.
Your marvelous doings are headline news;
I could write a book full of the details of
your greatness. (Psalm 145:1-6 MSG)

Dear God, You alone are so worthy of
every kind of praise. Amen.

WHY DOES EVIL HAPPEN?

We know that we are children of God and that the world around us is under the control of the evil one. And we know that the Son of God has come, and he has given us understanding so that we can know the true God. And now we live in fellowship with the true God because we live in fellowship with his Son, Jesus Christ. He is the only true God, and he is eternal life. Dear children, keep away from anything that might take God's place in your hearts.
1 JOHN 5:19–21 NLT

It's easy to get caught up in worry as we wonder why evil things happen in this world. It's because the whole world is under the power of the devil. But for all of us who believe in Jesus as Savior, we belong to God and the devil can never defeat us. The devil can attack us and hurt us, but God gives us life that lasts forever, no matter what! We should never want to follow any other type of false god who will lead us into the ways of the devil. Only the one true God leads us to life that lasts forever.

Dear God, I trust that with Jesus as my Savior— no matter what happens to me—You give me life that lasts forever! Please help me to share this truth with others so that they can be saved from the evil in this world too. Amen.

THINK ABOUT GOOD THINGS

Keep your minds thinking about whatever is true,
whatever is respected, whatever is right, whatever
is pure, whatever can be loved, and whatever is well
thought of. If there is anything good and worth
giving thanks for, think about these things.
PHILIPPIANS 4:8 NLV

God wants you to try to get rid of negative, worrisome thoughts and keep your mind thinking positively. When you focus on praise and gratitude to Him most of all—and on the many things that are right and true in your life—you keep your thoughts in the best places. When negative and nasty thoughts try to take over your mind, think of popping them like a bubble to make them disappear. Then let positive thought bubbles into your brain that are full of God's goodness and love. Remember Isaiah 26:3 (NLT), which says, "You will keep in perfect peace all who trust in you, all whose thoughts are fixed on you!"

Dear God, please help me to keep my brain
thinking about what is good for me—most of all
You, because You are so awesome! Amen.

ANGELS WATCHING OVER YOU

"Be sure you do not hate one of these little children. I tell you, they have angels who are always looking into the face of My Father in heaven."
MATTHEW 18:10 NLV

Maybe you hear people talk about guardian angels sometimes and wonder if they are real or not. This scripture in the Bible tells you that they are! So, when worries and fears are filling your mind, don't forget about angels. Ask God to send His help through them. Let these scriptures encourage you:

"The angel of the Lord stays close around those who fear Him, and He takes them out of trouble" (Psalm 34:7 NLV).

"I tell you, it is the same way among the angels of God. If one sinner is sorry for his sins and turns from them, the angels are very happy" (Luke 15:10 NLV).

"Keep on loving each other as Christian brothers. Do not forget to be kind to strangers and let them stay in your home. Some people have had angels in their homes without knowing it" (Hebrews 13:1–2 NLV).

Dear God, thank You for the angels You have assigned to protect and care for people! Amen.

DON'T SHOW OFF WITH PRAYER

*"When you pray, do not be as those who pretend
to be someone they are not. They love to stand and
pray in the places of worship or in the streets so
people can see them. For sure, I tell you, they have
all the reward they are going to get. When you pray,
go into a room by yourself. After you have shut the
door, pray to your Father Who is in secret. Then
your Father Who sees in secret will reward you."*

MATTHEW 6:5–6 NLV

Do you know any show-offs? How do you feel when you're
around them? Jesus talked about the kinds of people who
use prayer to show off, and He said not to be like them.
Our prayers should be a sincere conversation with our
heavenly Father, a time of praising Him and asking for His
help. Does this scripture passage mean that every single
prayer we pray should be said in secret when we're all
alone? No, but it is making the point that prayer should
be sincere and only to the one true God. And in every
prayer, we should want all attention on Him and His power
alone, not on ourselves.

*Dear God, help me never to want to put attention on
myself in prayer but to put all attention on You! Amen.*

WHEN WE MAKE BAD CHOICES, PART 1

And Jesus said, "There was a man who had two sons. The younger son said to his father, 'Father, let me have the part of the family riches that will be coming to me.' Then the father divided all that he owned between his two sons. Soon after that the younger son took all that had been given to him and went to another country far away. There he spent all he had on wild and foolish living. When all his money was spent, he was hungry. There was no food in the land. He went to work for a man in this far away country. His work was to feed pigs. He was so hungry he was ready to eat the outside part of the ears of the corn the pigs ate because no one gave him anything. He began to think about what he had done."
LUKE 15:11–17 NLV

In this parable, Jesus was teaching about God's great love for us, even when we make bad choices—just like the younger son in this story.

Dear God, please help me to think about my choices and admit to You when I've sinned against You. Please forgive me and help me not to make the same bad choices again in the future. Amen.

WHEN WE MAKE BAD CHOICES, PART 2

*"I will get up and go to my father. I
will say to him, 'Father, I have sinned
against heaven and against you.' "*

Luke 15:18 NLV

The parable from Jesus continues: "The son got up and went to his father. While he was yet a long way off, his father saw him. The father was full of loving-pity for him. He ran and threw his arms around him and kissed him. The son said to him, 'Father, I have sinned against heaven and against you. I am not good enough to be called your son.' But the father said to the workmen he owned, 'Hurry! Get the best coat and put it on him. Put a ring on his hand and shoes on his feet. Bring the calf that is fat and kill it. Let us eat and be glad. For my son was dead and now he is alive again. He was lost and now he is found. Let us eat and have a good time' " (Luke 15:20–24 NLV).

God loves us just like the father in the story loved his sons. He doesn't want to hold our sins against us. When we confess them to Him and come back to close relationship with Him, He feels like throwing us a big party too!

*Dear God, thank You so much for Your
amazing grace to forgive my sins. Amen.*

DON'T BE LIKE THEM

Do not want to be like those who do wrong. . . .
Trust in the Lord, and do good. So you will live
in the land and will be fed. Be happy in the Lord.
And He will give you the desires of your heart.
PSALM 37:1, 3–4 NLV

It's not always easy to stay away from those who are involved in doing things you know are wrong. Sometimes it seems fun and harmless to be like them and just go along with whatever seems popular, even if deep down you know it's not right. So, it takes courage to stay away from those doing wrong—especially if you're feeling pressure from people you thought were your friends. But God promises that if you trust Him and do good, you will have everything you need, and He will give you the things that make you happy because first you are happy in Him!

Dear God, please help me not want to be like
those who do wrong. Give me courage to do
what is wise and pleasing to You. I trust that's
the best way for me to be happy too. Amen.

LIKE A LION

*Those who are right with God have as
much strength of heart as a lion.*
PROVERBS 28:1 NLV

Believing in Jesus as the one who took away your sin
when He died on the cross is what makes you right with
God. And if you believe that and are living for Jesus, you
have as much strength of heart as a lion. That means your
heart and emotions can deal with any hard thing because
you know that real strength comes from God alone. He
is in you through His Holy Spirit. You can face any fear
or worry without running away because of God's great
power and love for you.

*Dear God, I trust in Jesus as my Savior from
sin, and I'm so grateful that makes me right
with You! Thank You for making me strong and
capable with Your awesome power. Amen.*

DON'T WORRY AND WHINE

*I waited patiently for the LORD; he
turned to me and heard my cry.*

PSALM 40:1 NIV

❀

Waiting for things to happen or for God to answer prayer can feel like forever and can be so frustrating and worrisome! But you can let God use those times to teach you to be patient and to depend on Him. Do you think it's fun to listen to someone whine and complain? Probably not. So, you want to be careful you don't do that either while you're waiting. Let these scriptures fill your mind and give you wisdom about waiting when you're feeling impatient:

"But they who wait upon the Lord will get new strength. They will rise up with wings like eagles. They will run and not get tired. They will walk and not become weak" (Isaiah 40:31 NLV).

"The Lord is good to those who wait for Him, to the one who looks for Him" (Lamentations 3:25 NLV).

*Dear God, please help me to wait like You want me
to—with patience and a good attitude. Help me not to
worry and whine. Please forgive me when I do. Amen.*

ALWAYS STRONGER

*The One Who lives in you is stronger
than the one who is in the world.*
1 JOHN 4:4 NLV

This is such a simple and powerful scripture to memorize and repeat when you're worried about anything. Our enemy, the devil, is stirring up all kinds of evil in this world. And you will be under attack from him sometimes, in all sorts of different ways—through anxiety attacks, through someone else's cruel words or actions, through stressful times for your family, through loss and sickness, and on and on. But no matter how strong the enemy and his evil seem against you and your loved ones, they are never stronger than the power of God in you through the Holy Spirit. Don't ever forget that. Call on God to help you be strong, peaceful, and patient and to help you see how He is working and taking care of you through it all.

*Dear God, deep down I know You are stronger
than anything that comes against me. But I
do forget that truth sometimes, and I'm sorry.
Please remind me, fill me with Your power and
peace, and do the fighting for me. Amen.*

THE WORD HELPS US DO WHAT'S RIGHT

Preach the Word of God. Preach it when it is easy
and people want to listen and when it is hard and
people do not want to listen. Preach it all the time.
Use the Word of God to show people they are wrong.
Use the Word of God to help them do right.

2 Timothy 4:2 NLV

The Bible will correct us if we read and listen to it, because it holds God's wisdom about what is right and what is wrong. This scripture reminds us that we need to use God's Word to show people when they are wrong and then help them do right according to God's Word. We need to keep sharing God's Word all the time, even when it's hard and people don't seem to want to listen. And, of course, we can't share it well unless we are constantly learning from it too. It shows us what we do wrong and what we need to correct in our own lives too.

Dear God, please give me wisdom and courage to
share Your Word and help people stop doing wrong and
instead do what is right—and that goes for me too!

DEEP ROOTS, PART 1

And now, just as you accepted Christ Jesus as your Lord, you must continue to follow him. Let your roots grow down into him, and let your lives be built on him. Then your faith will grow strong in the truth you were taught, and you will overflow with thankfulness.
COLOSSIANS 2:6–7 NLT

Memorize this scripture, and let it motivate you in your relationship with Jesus every day. The deeper your roots grow into Him, the sturdier your life is built on Him and the stronger your faith is in Him. And with deep roots, a sturdy life, and strong faith, the better you can fight off worries. You will still have them at times, of course, but they won't be able to totally overwhelm you. The stronger you are in relationship with Jesus, the more you will let Him take away your anxieties as you cast them on Him like His Word says to (1 Peter 5:7).

Dear God, help me to be like the sturdiest, tallest tree with my roots growing strong and deep into You. Amen.

DEEP ROOTS, PART 2

"A farmer went out to plant his seed. As he scattered it across his field, some seed fell on a footpath, where it was stepped on, and the birds ate it. Other seed fell among rocks. . .but the plant soon wilted and died for lack of moisture. Other seed fell among thorns that grew up with it and choked out the tender plants. Still other seed fell on fertile soil. . .and produced a crop that was a hundred times as much as had been planted!"
LUKE 8:5–8 NLT

Jesus told this parable to help us learn even more about having good, strong roots.

"The seed is God's word. The seeds that fell on the footpath represent those who hear the message, only to have the devil come and take it away from their hearts. . . . The seeds on the rocky soil represent those who hear the message and receive it with joy. But since they don't have deep roots, they believe for a while, then they fall away. . . . The seeds that fell among the thorns represent those who hear the message, but. . .the message is crowded out by the cares and riches and pleasures of this life. . . . And the seeds that fell on the good soil represent honest, good-hearted people who hear God's word, cling to it, and patiently produce a huge harvest" (Luke 8:11–15 NLT).

Dear God, help me to be that last kind of seed—one of the people with deep roots in You! Amen.

GOD'S RICHES AND POWER

God's riches are so great! The things He knows and His wisdom are so deep! No one can understand His thoughts. No one can understand His ways. The Holy Writings say, "Who knows the mind of the Lord? Who is able to tell Him what to do?" "Who has given first to God, that God should pay him back?" Everything comes from Him. His power keeps all things together. All things are made for Him. May He be honored forever. Let it be so.

ROMANS 11:33–36 NLV

God's riches, power, thoughts, and ways are so far above and beyond anything you can possibly imagine. So, pray big, telling God you know that nothing is impossible for Him and His power keeps all things together; yet also pray humbly, asking according to His will. And keep wanting God to grow your faith in Him, no matter if His answers to your prayers are what You hoped for or not.

Dear God, remind me to focus on how awesome You are, especially when I'm feeling worried. My mind can't fully understand You, but I want to grow closer to You and honor You. Please strengthen my faith in You and my relationship with You every day of my life. Amen.

TURN WAIT TIME INTO PRAYER TIME

Wait for the Lord. Be strong. Let your heart be strong. Yes, wait for the Lord.
PSALM 27:14 NLV

Sometimes you might be waiting on a big change in your life or help for a big decision, and it seems like nothing is happening. But God might be doing major work behind the scenes that you have no idea about. So, turn your wait times into more prayer time. Ask God to show you His plans and His purposes, and then wait patiently. You might be amazed by what He lets you see! And He might answer that He won't show you exactly what He's doing in your wait times, but you can pray for more trust in Him even when you can't see what He's doing. Your heavenly Father is always working for your good, whether you understand wait times or not. And you can always praise Him with gratitude for simply being His child.

Dear God, it's hard to wait and not know exactly how You might be working behind the scenes. But I trust You and love You, and I'm so thankful I am Yours. Amen.

LIVE IN PEACE

Do all that you can to live in peace with everyone.
ROMANS 12:18 NLT

Are you always at peace with your family and friends? Probably not. And that can cause lots of worries and stress. Any relationship is going to have some conflict sometimes, and that's okay if you work through it wisely! Physical fighting is not good, but conflict handled with wisdom can be really good—and we truly need it sometimes. But we shouldn't want to *stay* in conflict; we should work through it until there is peace again. James 4:1 (NLV) says, "What starts wars and fights among you? Is it not because you want many things and are fighting to have them?" This shows us that so many of our conflicts are caused by selfishness; and when we are willing to work to make peace, we should be willing to admit our own selfishness and mistakes even as we point out selfishness and mistakes in others.

Dear God, please show me how You want me to do my best to work to live in peace with everyone. Amen.

UNEXPECTED CHANGE OF PLANS

In their hearts humans plan their course,
but the LORD establishes their steps.
PROVERBS 16:9 NIV

Sometimes we make good plans, but they unexpectedly change, and we wonder why God doesn't help things turn out the way we thought they would or the way we planned. In those times, we must remember that God sees and knows all—far above and beyond what we can see. It's okay to make our plans (asking for God's wisdom and direction as we do), but we need to work toward them while also giving them to God, praying like this:

Dear God, I need Your wisdom and direction as I make plans. Please help my plans honor You and follow Your will. But please also help me to remember that You see things about my plans that I don't; and sometimes You change them or let changes happen to them. I might not always understand the details, but I trust You are doing what is best and will make everything right someday. Amen.

CELEBRITY STATUS, PART 1

The one who says he belongs to Christ should
live the same kind of life Christ lived.
1 JOHN 2:6 NLV

Do you have favorite celebrities? Are they athletes, actors, artists, social media stars, and/or musicians? What are all the things you know about them, and why are you a fan? Have you been to their games or concerts or shows? That's all fun if you also use wisdom about celebrities as you look up to them. We should never become so obsessed with celebrities to the point that we worship them. They are never perfect, and we can't forget that. Jesus is the one and only perfect famous person, and He alone should be worshipped. He alone should be the one we try to imitate.

Dear God, I want Jesus to be my first and
favorite person of influence. I want to worship
Him alone and live my life like Him. Amen.

CELEBRITY STATUS, PART 2

Follow my way of thinking as I follow Christ.
1 Corinthians 11:1 nlv

Far more important than having celebrities you admire is having mentors you admire. These are people who have lived longer than you who can help you through the stages of life ahead since they have already been there, done that. They should be people who love and follow Jesus so that they teach you more about loving and following Him too. If you're being realistic, you must admit you will likely never build a relationship with a famous celebrity—but you can definitely build a relationship with great personal mentors, who will be far more valuable to you than any celebrity. A personal mentor can be a part of your everyday life to help you mature and thrive.

Dear God, please send the right mentors into my life who love You and who will help teach and guide me to live like Jesus. Thank You! Amen.

SICKNESS AND HEALING

[Jesus] drove out the spirits with a
word and healed all the sick.
MATTHEW 8:16 NIV

When you're worried about an illness in yourself or a loved one, remember God's amazing power to heal! When Jesus was on earth, He showed that He truly was God with His incredible ability to heal people of sickness and demons. Jesus still has the power to heal today, and we can pray and ask God for healing when people need it. But we also need wisdom about it. Sometimes God chooses not to heal here on earth; but His healing in heaven is far better because it will last forever. So, even more important than praying for healing on earth is praying for people who don't know Jesus—that they come to know Him as Savior so that they can be healed in heaven with eternal life. As we pray for healing, we can do it with great faith, certain that God is absolutely able—but we must ask for it according to His will, knowing He always does what is right and good.

Dear Jesus, You have the power to heal and
perform any miracle, including healing from
any kind of sickness! Please give me wisdom
as I pray for Your will to be done. Amen.

WATCH YOUR WORDS

We can make a large horse go wherever we want by means of a small bit in its mouth. And a small rudder makes a huge ship turn wherever the pilot chooses to go, even though the winds are strong. In the same way, the tongue is a small thing that makes grand speeches. But a tiny spark can set a great forest on fire. And among all the parts of the body, the tongue is a flame of fire. It is a whole world of wickedness, corrupting your entire body. It can set your whole life on fire, for it is set on fire by hell itself.

JAMES 3:3–6 NLT

The Bible is clear that the words we speak are powerful, so we need to remember God's wisdom that we should be careful with them. Proverbs 21:23 (NLV) says, "He who watches over his mouth and his tongue keeps his soul from troubles." And Ephesians 4:29 (NLV) says, "Watch your talk! No bad words should be coming from your mouth. Say what is good. Your words should help others grow as Christians."

Dear God, please help me to remember that the words I say matter, and they are powerful. Please help me to use my words wisely. Amen.

LOVE AND DISCIPLINE, PART 1

*"Don't make light of the LORD's discipline,
and don't give up when he corrects you. For
the LORD disciplines those he loves, and he
punishes each one he accepts as his child."*
HEBREWS 12:5–6 NLT

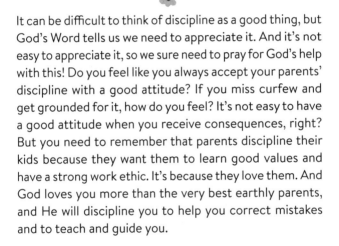

It can be difficult to think of discipline as a good thing, but God's Word tells us we need to appreciate it. And it's not easy to appreciate it, so we sure need to pray for God's help with this! Do you feel like you always accept your parents' discipline with a good attitude? If you miss curfew and get grounded for it, how do you feel? It's not easy to have a good attitude when you receive consequences, right? But you need to remember that parents discipline their kids because they want them to learn good values and have a strong work ethic. It's because they love them. And God loves you more than the very best earthly parents, and He will discipline you to help you correct mistakes and to teach and guide you.

Dear God, remind me that You are always loving me perfectly, even if I don't always understand or enjoy what You're doing. Please help me to appreciate that You correct and guide me with good discipline! Amen.

LOVE AND DISCIPLINE, PART 2

As you endure this divine discipline, remember
that God is treating you as his own children.
HEBREWS 12:7 NLT

Unfortunately, it's easy to find parents who don't discipline their kids much at all. Their lack of discipline often shows up in stressful and chaotic ways in these families' lives. If you can observe this kind of thing wisely, you'll realize why discipline is good and also loving. Hebrews 12 goes on to tell us why: "God's discipline is always good for us, so that we might share in his holiness. No discipline is enjoyable while it is happening—it's painful! But afterward there will be a peaceful harvest of right living for those who are trained in this way" (Hebrews 12:10–11 NLT).

Dear God, I want to share in Your holiness, and I
want the peaceful life that comes from being trained
by discipline. So please remind me in the middle of
discipline I don't enjoy that these are the things You're
doing in my life. I am so grateful to be Your child! Amen.

DON'T WORRY ABOUT FEELING WEIRD

*Dear friends, your real home is not here on
earth. You are strangers here. I ask you to keep
away from all the sinful desires of the flesh.
These things fight to get hold of your soul.*
1 PETER 2:11 NLV

It feels weird to be a Christian sometimes—and that's a
good thing, because God's Word tells us we should. So,
don't worry about it! Some versions of 1 Peter 2:11 describe
Christians as being like aliens here on earth in the sense
that we are strangers here because this world is not our
real home. When we believe in Jesus as Savior, we know
that He will give us eternal life someday in heaven, which *is*
our real home. So, we should be careful not to follow what
the world says is good and popular but instead follow what
God says is good—which will often be unpopular in the
world. This will help show others the difference following
Jesus makes, and hopefully they will want to follow Him
too. Being a Christian in this world isn't always easy, but
it is always totally worth it!

*Dear God, no matter how weird I feel, help me to
follow Your ways and wisdom above all—because I
know my real home is in heaven with You. Amen.*

THE LORD KNOWS IT ALL

O Lord, You have looked through me and have known me. You know when I sit down and when I get up. You understand my thoughts from far away. You look over my path and my lying down. You know all my ways very well. Even before I speak a word, O Lord, You know it all. You have closed me in from behind and in front. And You have laid Your hand upon me. All You know is too great for me. It is too much for me to understand.
PSALM 139:1–6 NLV

You can never keep a secret from God. Not ever. He knows absolutely everything. Even before you say a word, God knows you're going to say it. He knows every single one of your thoughts and always knows exactly what you're doing—even where and when. To some people, that might seem stressful, but for those who love God and want a good relationship with Him through Jesus, it never has to be. God loves you! And because He sees and knows everything about you, you should feel greatly loved, protected, and cared for.

Dear God, thank You for loving me so much that You know absolutely everything about me! Amen.

GOD KEEPS HIS WORD

"God is not a man, that He should lie. He is not a son of man, that He should be sorry for what He has said. Has He said, and will He not do it? Has He spoken, and will He not keep His Word?"
NUMBERS 23:19 NLV

Only God will never break a promise. He is the only one who can make a perfect promise. He will always keep His Word. He is not human, and He cannot lie or make mistakes. When He speaks, He is always right and true. Even the very best people, who love you the most, will let you down sometimes even when they don't mean to—because they are human. But God is above and beyond us, and you can trust Him completely. So, give Him all your worries today and every day, and trust that He will give you His peace in return.

Dear God, thank You for being the very best promise keeper! I want to keep reading Your Word and drawing closer to You—my stability and strength—through everything in life. Amen.

GOD WRECKS BAD PLANS

*The Lord brings the plans of nations to nothing.
He wrecks the plans of the people. The plans of
the Lord stand forever. The plans of His heart
stand through the future of all people. Happy
is the nation whose God is the Lord. Happy are
the people He has chosen for His own.*
PSALM 33:10–12 NLV

Are you worried that someone might have evil plans to embarrass or hurt you in some way? Hopefully not; but if you ever are, then remember this scripture from Psalm 33. God wrecks the plans of people if He wants to. He can wreck any bad plan that someone might have against you. And if He does allow something bad to happen to you, He has plans to make you stronger because of it and turn it into something good instead. Romans 8:28 (NLV) promises: "God makes all things work together for the good of those who love Him and are chosen to be a part of His plan."

*Dear God, I believe You can wreck any bad plan or
turn it into good somehow, so I never need to worry.
Your plans are always the best, and I trust You! Amen.*

YOUR HELP COMES FROM THE LORD

I will lift up my eyes to the mountains. Where will my help come from? My help comes from the Lord, Who made heaven and earth. He will not let your feet go out from under you. He Who watches over you will not sleep. Listen, He Who watches over Israel will not close his eyes or sleep. The Lord watches over you. The Lord is your safe cover at your right hand. The sun will not hurt you during the day and the moon will not hurt you during the night. The Lord will keep you from all that is sinful. He will watch over your soul. The Lord will watch over your coming and going, now and forever.
PSALM 121:1–8 NLV

Never forget that every bit of help you get ultimately comes from God. He is the one watching over you always and providing the people and resources you need at just the right time. Praise and thank Him every time you ask for help and receive it and for all the ways you are helped without ever having to ask!

Dear God, everything good comes from You! I can never thank You enough for the countless ways You help me every day. Amen.

DON'T GET TIRED OF DOING GOOD

*So let's not get tired of doing what is good. At just
the right time we will reap a harvest of blessing
if we don't give up. Therefore, whenever we have
the opportunity, we should do good to everyone—
especially to those in the family of faith.*
GALATIANS 6:9–10 NLT

If we're not careful, it is super easy to get tired of doing
good and making the right choices to obey God. Our
enemy wants us to believe it's too hard, too exhausting,
to follow Jesus. Making bad choices and acting selfishly
seem to be the easy, comfortable way a lot of the time.
And sometimes it is a lot easier—at first—but in the long
run, it will cause us all kinds of anxiety and consequences.
God's ways are *always* best for us. And He will help us not
get worn out if we ask Him. He can give us everything
we need for doing the good things He has planned for us.

*Dear God, help me to find everything I
need in You so that I don't ever get tired of
doing good and never give up. Amen.*

WHEN YOU JUST DON'T KNOW

*The Holy Spirit helps us in our weakness. For example,
we don't know what God wants us to pray for. But the
Holy Spirit prays for us with groanings that cannot
be expressed in words. And the Father who knows all
hearts knows what the Spirit is saying, for the Spirit
pleads for us believers in harmony with God's own will.*
ROMANS 8:26–27 NLT

Sometimes it's so hard to know exactly what to pray for
in a difficult situation you or a loved one is experiencing.
So, we can be thankful that the Bible tells us the Holy
Spirit prays and communicates for us, taking our words
and explaining them to God in exactly the best way. And
God promises to work out everything according to His
will and for our good.

When you're feeling unsure how to pray, tell God exactly
that and then keep on praying. Ask the Holy Spirit to take
your words and make them the best they can be before
God, who loves you and will work out His perfect plans.

*Dear God, I'm not always sure what to say to You, but
I never want to stop talking to You in prayer. Amen.*

WORRIES ARE FOR ONLY A LITTLE WHILE

*After you have suffered for awhile, God Himself
will make you perfect. He will keep you in the
right way. He will give you strength. He is the God
of all loving-favor and has called you through
Christ Jesus to share His shining-greatness
forever. God has power over all things forever.*
1 PETER 5:10–11 NLV

You know there are all kinds of worries and hurts in this
world—little ones and big ones. But God's Word promises
that all kinds of suffering and pain are just for a little while
in this world and that perfection awaits us in heaven.
Meanwhile, God will keep you on the right path and give
you strength to deal with the stress and hardship of this
life. No hardship can ever overpower you because you
trust that God has power over all things.

*Dear Jesus, I hate the stressful and painful things of
this world, but I love that You have complete power
over all of them. I believe that You are working to
make all things perfect and worry-free forever in
heaven—for me and all who trust in You. Amen.*

FORGIVE LIKE GOD DOES

*"When you stand to pray, if you have anything
against anyone, forgive him. Then your Father
in heaven will forgive your sins also. If you
do not forgive them their sins, your Father
in heaven will not forgive your sins."*
MARK 11:25–26 NLV

When we're praying and wanting God to pay attention,
we need God's forgiveness of our sins. And we also need
to forgive others for their sins that have caused us hurt.
God loves giving grace and forgiveness, and He wants us
to copy Him. We should be so grateful for forgiveness
of our own sin that we offer forgiveness generously to
others, just like God does.

This can be very hard to do. Think of a time when someone mistreated you. It's awful! But with God's power
working in you, offering forgiveness is always possible.
Even if someone who has hurt you doesn't ever seem sorry
and you might never be close friends, you can still ask
God to help you let go of the anger and pain they caused
and trust that He is working all things out for good.

*Dear God, I need Your help to copy forgiveness the
way You give it so kindly and generously. Amen.*

WHEN YOU'RE WEARY FROM WORRIES

*Have you not known? Have you not heard? The God
Who lives forever is the Lord, the One Who made the
ends of the earth. He will not become weak or tired. His
understanding is too great for us to begin to know. He
gives strength to the weak. And He gives power to him
who has little strength. Even very young men get tired
and become weak and strong young men trip and fall.
But they who wait upon the Lord will get new strength.
They will rise up with wings like eagles. They will run and
not get tired. They will walk and not become weak.*
ISAIAH 40:28–31 NLV

Even the very best GOATs—the athletes considered the
greatest of all time—here on earth get tired and need
their sleep. They don't have endless energy and strength,
no matter how much they run and lift weights and train.
Only God never becomes tired or weak, and this scripture
in Isaiah can encourage you when you feel weary from all
your worries. Pray to God and wait for Him. He is your
source of true energy, strength, and peace.

*Dear God, thank You that You never tire and
that You give me peace and strength and
energy exactly when I need it. Amen.*

THE WORLD'S WISDOM VS. GOD'S WISDOM

*If you have jealousy in your heart and fight to
have many things, do not be proud of it. Do not
lie against the truth. This is not the kind of wisdom
that comes from God. But this wisdom comes from
the world and from that which is not Christian and
from the devil. . . . The wisdom that comes from
heaven is first of all pure. Then it gives peace.*
JAMES 3:14–15, 17 NLV

James 3 helps us know what real wisdom from God looks
like in our lives. It's very different from worldly wisdom. In fact, 1 Corinthians 3:19 (NLV) says, "The wisdom
of this world is foolish to God." So, it's important for us
always to be praying to know the difference between
the world's kind of wisdom and God's real wisdom. And
we can only do that by constantly learning from God's
Word and asking Him to show us how to use it in our lives
through the power of the Holy Spirit, who lives in us if we
have committed our lives to Jesus as our Lord and Savior.

*Dear God, please keep giving me Your real
wisdom that brings peace, and help me see the
big difference from the world's wisdom. Amen.*

THE VOICE OF THE LORD

The voice of the LORD echoes above the sea.
The God of glory thunders.
The LORD thunders over the mighty sea.
The voice of the LORD is powerful;
the voice of the LORD is majestic.
The voice of the LORD splits the mighty cedars;
the LORD shatters the cedars of Lebanon. . . .
The voice of the LORD strikes
with bolts of lightning.
PSALM 29:3–5, 7 NLT

No one has power to help you with any worry or stress like God does. Let this scripture from Psalm 29 encourage you. Read it, remember it, and trust in it—and let it grow your faith in our extraordinary God. With just His voice, God can do anything at all. No matter what is going on in the world, God is always in control, always able to use His voice to help and rescue you in the good ways He chooses.

Dear God, remind me of the power of Your
incredible voice that can do anything at all
to help me and give me peace! Amen.

KEEP GROWING IN YOUR GIFTS

*Do your best to improve your faith by adding
goodness, understanding, self-control, patience,
devotion to God, concern for others, and love. If
you keep growing in this way, it will show that
what you know about our Lord Jesus Christ
has made your lives useful and meaningful.*
2 PETER 1:5–8 CEV

You might be super social, or you might be on the quiet
side. Both are wonderful! What matters is that you're aware
of how God made you and that you ask Him to help you
use the personality and the gifts He's given you to serve
Him. He can continually grow and develop you with new
traits and gifts and skills according to His will, so let Him!
But to do these things the best way, you need to stay in
constant good relationship and communication with Him.
So never stop praying. Never stop reading God's Word.
Never stop learning from and serving your loving Father!

*Dear God, help me to learn more about myself
and how You designed me, as I keep learning
from You and staying close to You. Amen.*

GET YOUR REST, PART 1

*By the seventh day God had finished the work he
had been doing; so on the seventh day he rested
from all his work. Then God blessed the seventh
day and made it holy, because on it he rested
from all the work of creating that he had done.*

GENESIS 2:2–3 NIV

Getting enough rest really is a big deal; and when we
don't get enough rest, any worry and stress and anxiety
in life often feel so much worse because we're too tired
to handle it well. God thought rest was such a big deal
that He set aside an entire day of the week for it! Rest is
necessary for your physical health in many ways, and it's
necessary for your spiritual health too. God intends rest
for both actual sleeping and for time simply spent with
Him, relaxing while you focus on how great He is and how
much He loves you!

*Dear God, please help me to be thankful for rest
time rather than annoyed by it. You designed it,
and it's so good for me. Thank You! Amen.*

GET YOUR REST, PART 2

*"Come to me, all you who are weary and burdened,
and I will give you rest. Take my yoke upon you
and learn from me, for I am gentle and humble
in heart, and you will find rest for your souls.
For my yoke is easy and my burden is light."*
MATTHEW 11:28–30 NIV

God doesn't want you to be constantly busy and stressed and exhausted. He wants you to be full of His peace, and for that you need plenty of sleep and plenty of time spent learning from Him, worshipping Him, and praying to Him. Let these scriptures help you learn even more about how important good rest is to God:

"The followers of Jesus came back to Him. They told Jesus all they had done and taught. He said to them, 'Come away from the people. Be by yourselves and rest'" (Mark 6:30–31 NLV).

"Be quiet and know that I am God. I will be honored among the nations. I will be honored in the earth" (Psalm 46:10–11 NLV).

*Dear God, please help these verses stick in my
mind forever to remind me of how important it is
to rest well and especially to rest in You! Amen.*

CRY TO THE LORD IN YOUR TROUBLE

*I cried to the Lord in my trouble, and He
answered me and put me in a good place.*
PSALM 118:5 NLV

When you feel like you're in a whole lot of trouble, stop to think about how God has helped you out of trouble in the past. This will help calm you down as you trust that He will help you again. Psalm 118 encourages us that we can always cry out to God in our trouble, and He will help us get back into a good, safe place. The scripture continues,

"The Lord is with me. I will not be afraid of what man can do to me. The Lord is with me. He is my Helper. I will watch those lose who fight against me. It is better to trust in the Lord than to trust in man. It is better to trust in the Lord than to trust in rulers" (Psalm 118:6–9).

Dear Lord, I trust You more than any person or leader. I know You are always with me, and I don't need to be afraid of anyone or anything. When I'm in trouble, please help me to get out of it and get into a good, safe place. Thank You! Amen.

DON'T FALL FOR FAKE GODS

Our God is in the heavens. He does whatever He wants to do. Their gods are silver and gold, the work of human hands. They have mouths but they cannot speak. They have eyes but they cannot see. They have ears but they cannot hear. They have noses but they cannot smell. They have hands but they cannot feel. They have feet but they cannot walk. They cannot make a sound come out of their mouths. Those who make them and trust them will be like them.

PSALM 115:3–8 NLV

This scripture compares our one true God with the fake gods of the world that some people create for themselves. Fake gods are absurd, with useless mouths, eyes, ears, noses, hands, and feet. But people often make fake gods because they don't really want to serve or worship anyone but themselves. It's all useless. But to trust, worship, and obey the one true God alone is to live the life you were created for with love, hope, and perfect peace that lasts forever.

Dear God, please help me never to fall for a fake god. I'm so thankful I trust in You, the one true God! Help me to live for You and do the good things You created me for. Amen.

LET FAITH HEROES ENCOURAGE YOU

*Faith makes us sure of what we hope for and gives
us proof of what we cannot see. It was their faith
that made our ancestors pleasing to God.*
HEBREWS 11:1–2 CEV

We can get so much encouragement from the lives of
people with great faith who have gone before us. Hebrews
11 is a wonderful chapter of the Bible to help us remember a whole list of faith heroes—people like Noah and
Moses and Joseph and Sarah and Rahab, who continued
to believe in God and His promises even during the most
difficult times. Like them, we should want to hold on to
our faith, no matter what. Think about the people among
your family and friends who have incredible faith in God,
those who are still living and those who have passed away.
Keep looking up to and honoring them and their example
now and every day of your life too!

*Dear God, when I'm feeling stressed and
worried, please help me to be encouraged by
everyone who has gone before me and had
great faith in You, no matter what. Amen.*

PRAISE GOD FOR CREATION

*"You are worthy, O Lord our God, to receive glory
and honor and power. For you created all things, and
they exist because you created what you pleased."*
REVELATION 4:11 NLT

Think of your favorite amusement park. Or what's your favorite city to visit? What God made people capable of designing and building for others to enjoy is pretty amazing, isn't it? But none of it compares with the beauty and awesomeness of God's creation, though! Only God can create incredible natural wonders. What is your favorite part of God's creation?

A wonderful way to deal with worry is to get outside and spend time enjoying nature. Pray to God with gratitude and praise for the beauty all around you. Then let Him fill you with His powerful peace.

*Dear God, You are so awesome to have created
such a beautiful world for us to live and grow
in. Draw me closer to You as I take pleasure
in everything You have made. Amen.*

EQUALITY

For you are all children of God through faith in Christ Jesus. And all who have been united with Christ in baptism have put on Christ, like putting on new clothes. There is no longer Jew or Gentile, slave or free, male and female. For you are all one in Christ Jesus.
GALATIANS 3:26–28 NLT

We hear the word *equality* a lot these days, and it's stressful to figure out who to listen to about it. We need wisdom about who alone gives real equality—it's Jesus! Because of sin in the world, people will never get equality exactly right. There will always be bad people trying to say some groups of people are better than others. But don't ever listen to or join them. In God's eyes, because of Jesus, every single person is the same in value. We all matter so much to God that He sent Jesus to die to save us from our sins. And when anyone trusts in Jesus, they become a child of the one true God, the King of all kings. That makes us all equally royal, and we should want to share this awesome truth with everyone we can!

Dear God, You offer the only true equality through Jesus. Thank You that anyone can be Your child by trusting that only Jesus saves. Help me to share Your love and truth and wisdom. Amen.

PRAY IN PUBLIC

*Remember to pray for all Christians. Pray for me
also. Pray that I might open my mouth without fear.*
EPHESIANS 6:18–19 NLV

Do you have a favorite coffee shop or café? Do you ever
see people in those kinds of places reading their Bibles
and praying? It's so encouraging! Since we are Christians
in the USA, where we are totally free to worship and pray
to God in public, we should be doing this as much as
possible. There are Christians all around the world who
live in places where it's very dangerous to openly follow
Jesus. Unless we've been there, it's hard to imagine how
awful that must be. They desperately need our prayers
all the time. And even more, because they cannot pray
in public, we should be grateful we never have to hide
our faith or our prayers. We should gladly share our faith
and our prayers, even if it's simply bowing our heads and
praying sincerely and humbly before a meal in a public
place—giving thanks to our one true God and our Savior,
Jesus Christ.

*Dear God, help me to gladly pray to You and read my
Bible in public places. I pray for Your extra closeness
and care for those Christians all around the world
who are in great danger because they follow You.
Protect them and strengthen them, please! Amen.*

ABOVE ALL ELSE

*Guard your heart above all else, for it
determines the course of your life.*
P<small>ROVERBS</small> 4:23 <small>NLT</small>

If you feel worried some of the time, that's understandable.
But what if you feel worried *all* the time? Not good! You
need to figure out where that constant confusing and
overwhelming anxiety is coming from and how to communicate about it, plus hopefully work out what's causing
it. Ask your parents and other trusted adults for help, and
be totally honest about your feelings. Never forget that
God knows your heart best of all, and He can help you with
everything you feel. Pray to Him and ask Him to give you
great wisdom when it comes to your thoughts, emotions,
and actions and how they all interact.

*Dear God, sometimes I'm worrying so much that I'm
not sure what to do with it all. You know my heart and
every thought and feeling even better than I do. Can
You please help me sort them out and communicate
them well so others can help me? Thank You! Amen.*

WAIT PATIENTLY

*I wait for the Lord. My soul waits
and I hope in His Word.*
PSALM 130:5 NLV

When we feel like God is taking way too long to answer our prayers, we can find comfort and peace in the fact that the prophet Habakkuk felt impatient too. He prayed, "O Lord, how long must I call for help before You will hear? I cry out to You, 'We are being hurt!' But You do not save us" (Habakkuk 1:2 NLV).

And we can learn from God's response that our human minds can never fully know and understand what God is doing when it feels like He's taking much too long to answer our prayers: "Look among the nations, and see! Be surprised and full of wonder! For I am doing something in your days that you would not believe if you were told" (Habakkuk 1:5 NLV).

*Dear God, help me to remember that just because
I feel impatient, that doesn't mean You are not
working out Your plans in exactly the right ways. You
are good, and I trust You and hope in You. Amen.*

SPEAK THE TRUTH

The LORD detests lying lips, but he delights
in those who tell the truth.
PROVERBS 12:22 NLT

Being honest about everything will help you avoid all kinds of stress and anxiety in life. If you make honesty and integrity a top priority, you will be known as a trustworthy person. Bosses, leaders, and teachers notice consistent honesty, and good ones usually want to reward us and give new opportunities because of it. Luke 16:10–12 (NLV) says, "He that is faithful with little things is faithful with big things also. He that is not honest with little things is not honest with big things. If you have not been faithful with riches of this world, who will trust you with true riches? If you have not been faithful in that which belongs to another person, who will give you things to have as your own?"

Dear God, I want You to delight in me because I
always tell the truth. I want to be wise, honest,
and trustworthy in all things. Amen.

WATCH FOR JESUS TO RETURN

*We are to be looking for the great hope
and the coming of our great God and
the One Who saves, Christ Jesus.*

Titus 2:13 NLV

We should always be watching for Jesus to return because He promised He would! The idea of Jesus returning might sound a little scary, because it will be unlike anything any person has ever experienced. But for those who love and trust Him, His return will be wonderful, and we should have great excitement and hope about it! Mark 13:24–27 (NLV) says, "After those days of much trouble and pain and sorrow are over, the sun will get dark. The moon will not give light. The stars will fall from the sky. The powers in the heavens will be shaken. Then they will see the Son of Man coming in the clouds with great power and shining-greatness. He will send His angels. They will gather together God's people from the four winds. They will come from one end of the earth to the other end of heaven."

*Dear Jesus, I'm watching and waiting for You
to return and gather Your people, including
me! I love You and trust You! Amen.*

GO TO GOD MOST HIGH, ALL-POWERFUL

Those who go to God Most High for safety
will be protected by God All-Powerful.
PSALM 91:1 ICB

Never forget who your God is—the all-powerful one! This scripture in Psalm 91 continues:

I will say to the Lord, "You are my place of safety and protection. You are my God, and I trust you." God will save you from hidden traps and from deadly diseases. He will protect you like a bird spreading its wings over its young. His truth will be like your armor and shield. You will not fear any danger by night or an arrow during the day. You will not be afraid of diseases that come in the dark or sickness that strikes at noon (Psalm 91:2–6 ICB).

There is power in knowing and praying God's Word when you feel overcome with worry about things you cannot control. Remember that God *can* control all of it, and He loves you like crazy. Keep trusting in His love and talking to Him about everything!

Dear God, this world can be so weird and scary.
I need You to remind me how much bigger You
are than any evil thing and how You love and
protect me. I come to You for safety and peace,
and I know You'll give it generously. Amen.

LEARN FROM MARY AND MARTHA, PART 1

Jesus said to her, "Martha, Martha, you are worried and troubled about many things. Only a few things are important, even just one. Mary has chosen the good thing. It will not be taken away from her."
LUKE 10:38–41 NLV

Martha and Mary were good friends of Jesus, and the story of the time they had Him over for dinner can help us deal with anxiety. Martha was keeping very busy doing good things to make a nice meal and take care of Jesus. But she was worried and upset that her sister, Mary, wasn't helping enough. Can you relate? Do you ever feel like you're the one doing all the work when others are supposed to be helping you? It's frustrating and stressful, for sure! But in this case, Jesus gently told Martha that Mary was doing the very best thing—listening to His teaching. Our worries will be eased if we simply sit still and listen to Jesus too.

Dear Jesus, please remind me that fussing and fretting over everything being perfect is not good for me. It's far more important to spend time with You and listen to what You want to teach me. Amen.

LEARN FROM MARY AND MARTHA, PART 2

Don't just listen to God's word. You must do what it says. Otherwise, you are only fooling yourselves.
JAMES 1:22 NLT

We could take this story of Martha and Mary too far and use it as an excuse for laziness. But that's not right! God created you to do good things, and that requires getting out of bed or off the couch! When we use wisdom, we realize there's a balance between *hearing* God's Word and *doing* what it says, and that balance can only happen if we put listening to and following Jesus at the top of our to-do list. Everything else we need to do should come after that number-one priority!

Dear Jesus, please help me always to find the right balance of listening to You and following Your Word, plus doing the good things You have created me for. Amen.

KEEP ASKING

Jesus said to them, "If one of you has a friend and goes to him in the night and says, 'Friend, give me three loaves of bread, for a friend of mine is on a trip and has stopped at my house. I have no food to give him.' The man inside the house will say, 'Do not trouble me'. . . . I say to you, he may not get up and give him bread because he is a friend. Yet, if he keeps on asking, he will get up and give him as much as he needs. I say to you, ask, and what you ask for will be given to you. Look, and what you are looking for you will find. Knock, and the door you are knocking on will be opened to you. For everyone who asks, will receive what he asks for. Everyone who looks, will find what he is looking for. Everyone who knocks, will have the door opened to him."
LUKE 11:5–10 NLV

Do you wonder if God ever gets tired of you asking for things in prayer? Jesus Himself taught in the Bible that God absolutely does not! He is your all-powerful, never-tiring heavenly Father, and in Luke 11, Jesus tells you to keep on asking!

Dear God, thank You for wanting me to ask You for what I need over and over and over again. Amen.

139

FIGHT WORRY WITH WISDOM

*If you do not have wisdom, ask God for it. He is
always ready to give it to you and will never say
you are wrong for asking. You must have faith as
you ask Him. You must not doubt. Anyone who
doubts is like a wave which is pushed around by the
sea. Such a man will get nothing from the Lord.*

JAMES 1:5–7 NLV

Sometimes we must wait on God to give us what we ask
for, but James 1:5 tells us something God is always ready
to give us—*wisdom!* And we sure do need God's wisdom
in this crazy world that gives us so many things to worry
about. So much that is popular in our culture goes against
the good truth and guidance of God's Word. So every
day—every *minute!*—ask God to give you His wisdom. Have
faith, and never doubt that He will give it to you. Then use
that wisdom in every area of your life!

*Dear God, thank You for being so generous with wisdom.
I need it every minute, and I'm asking You again now.
I believe You'll give it and guide me with it. Amen.*

TRADE WORRY FOR PRAYER AND PEACE

"Peace I leave with you."
JOHN 14:27 NIV

Among many verses in the Bible that tell us not to worry or be afraid, some of the best are Jesus' words in John 14:27: "Peace I leave with you. My peace I give to you. I do not give peace to you as the world gives. Do not let your hearts be troubled or afraid" (John 14:27 NLV). And Psalm 55:22 (NLV) says, "Give all your cares to the Lord and He will give you strength. He will never let those who are right with Him be shaken."

Every person, family, relationship, and situation have unique challenges and troubles, and it's super hard not to worry about them. But you can train your brain to take those worrisome thoughts, give them over to God in prayer, and let Him replace them with His truth and peace.

Dear God, worries steal my peace and trust in You. Please take each worry from my mind, and replace it with a powerful and soothing truth about Your strength, Your protection, Your love, and Your blessing for me. Amen.

BE A PROACTIVE PRAYER

Look to the Lord and ask for His strength.
Look to Him all the time.
1 CHRONICLES 16:11 NLV

Some people pray only as a reaction to life's negative events—like only praying to God when you're already sick rather than also praying ahead of time to stay healthy. Or only praying to God in emergency situations or natural disasters rather than praying to God all the time in relationship with Him. Of course, we should pray in reaction to life's events. We sure need God's help! But we should also be strongly *proactive* in our prayers, building a close relationship with God while talking with Him all the time about everything—past, present, and future—not just when we find ourselves in desperate need of help

Dear God, help me to be a proactive prayer who
loves to talk to You in all kinds of situations. Amen.

POSITION OF PRAYER

*Then Ezra praised the L*ORD*, the great God, and all
the people chanted, "Amen! Amen!" as they lifted
their hands. Then they bowed down and worshiped
the L*ORD *with their faces to the ground.*

NEHEMIAH 8:6 NLT

When we pray, it's often with bowed heads, closed eyes,
and folded hands. But there is no specific position you must
pray in because you never have to stop praying to God.
You can be sitting, standing, or raising your hands, and you
can be anywhere at all when you pray. But sometimes it's
good to position your body in a way that reminds you of
God's utter greatness and your total respect for, devotion
to, and need for Him.

*Dear God, help me to remember that I can pray to
You anywhere I am, but I also want to remember to
bow and kneel before You at times to show You how
much I respect, love, and need You. I am so grateful
to be a child of the King of all kings! I worship You, my
Creator, my Savior, and my awesome God! Amen.*

DON'T GET REVENGE

*Never pay back evil with more evil. Do things in such
a way that everyone can see you are honorable.
Do all that you can to live in peace with everyone.
Dear friends, never take revenge. Leave that to the
righteous anger of God. For the Scriptures say, "I will
take revenge; I will pay them back," says the LORD.*
ROMANS 12:17–19 NLT

Our instant reaction to being mistreated is usually to
want to mistreat the person right back. If someone calls
us nasty names, we want to call them nasty names too.
If someone lies about us, we want to lie about them too.
But that's not what God's Word tells us to do. God wants
us to let Him handle our mistreatment. He will do things
with perfect justice in a way that we never could. Our job
is never to pay back evil with evil, but instead to live in a
way that others see we are honorable and that we try to
live at peace with everyone.

*Dear God, it's so hard not to want to get revenge all on
my own, but please help me to stay calm and let You
handle it with Your perfect ways and plans. Amen.*

PAY THEM BACK WITH BLESSING

*Don't repay evil for evil. Don't retaliate with
insults when people insult you. Instead, pay them
back with a blessing. That is what God has called
you to do, and he will grant you his blessing.*
1 PETER 3:9 NLT

Even though it feels awful when someone is treating you
cruelly, you can choose to learn from the experience
instead of letting it make you depressed or full of anxiety.
You can learn what *not* to do to someone else. You can
learn to choose better. God wants us to take that higher
road and not seek revenge on people who mistreat us. In
fact, He wants us to instead pray that blessings will come
to the people who do bad things to us. That's hard—but
remember that God wants to bless you when you obey
His wisdom. Ask Him to help you, and then see how He
rewards you!

*Dear God, I pray for those who treat me badly.
Please help them to stop and come to know You
as Savior. Help them want to share Your love.
Please bless them with good things to fill their lives.
Help me not to want revenge. Instead, help me to
trust in You to take care of everything. Amen.*

LOVE COVERS A MULTITUDE OF SINS

Most important of all, continue to show deep love for each other, for love covers a multitude of sins.
1 PETER 4:8 NLT

When we find ourselves fighting with a loved one and dealing with a relationship that seems broken, it's upsetting. Rifts in relationships often happen because we're not giving enough patience to one another, we're not listening well, or we're letting selfishness take over. But conflict can be worked out and the relationship can be restored if we stay humble and ask for God's help. We can pray, *God, please forgive us and help us forgive each other, and cover our mistakes with Your love and grace.* Once we pray like that, we can communicate better in peaceful ways and then move forward in trying to figure out what's causing our conflict and unkind words and actions.

Dear Jesus, thank You for Your great love. You covered all our sin with Your blood when You took sin upon Yourself and died on the cross. You didn't deserve to die, but that's how much You love us! Help us to model Your great love and grace with each other. Amen.

CHOOSE A GOOD REPUTATION

Choose a good reputation over great riches;
being held in high esteem is better than silver
or gold. . . . True humility and fear of the
Lord lead to riches, honor, and long life.
PROVERBS 22:1, 4 NLT

When people hear your name, do you want them to think of you in good ways or bad ways? Do you want to be known for things like laziness or lying or rudeness or getting into trouble? Or do you want to be known for things like doing your best and being honest, fair, kind, and worthy of respect? Be intentional. Do your very best to have excellent character and a good reputation your whole life. It doesn't mean you will always be perfect, but it means you will live for God and obey His ways of love, fairness, and honesty—and you will quickly want to make things right when you make a mistake and do wrong.

Dear God, I want to be known for good character
and a good name because I obey You. Please keep
me on the right paths, always following You. Amen.

STRESSFUL STUFF

"Do not gather together for yourself riches of this earth. They will be eaten by bugs and become rusted. Men can break in and steal them. Gather together riches in heaven where they will not be eaten by bugs or become rusted. Men cannot break in and steal them. For wherever your riches are, your heart will be there also."
MATTHEW 6:19–21 NLV

Stuff easily piles up, and sometimes having too much stuff causes us anxiety and we need to get rid of some things. Jesus taught us to be careful, because we should be storing up riches for ourselves in heaven, not on earth. We can't take any of our stuff from earth to heaven with us, so we shouldn't get too caught up in having it here on earth. What does it mean to gather riches in heaven? It means that God will be rewarding us with blessings that last forever—these rewards are based on the good things we are doing now to bring glory to Him here on earth.

Dear God, help me to want treasures in heaven much more than any collection of treasures here on earth. Help me to use wisdom about what stuff I keep and what stuff I get rid of. Amen.

PRAY LIKE DANIEL PRAYED

*Three times a day [Daniel] got down on
his knees and prayed, giving thanks to his
God, just as he had done before.*
DANIEL 6:10 NIV

Daniel in the lions' den isn't just a little kids' Sunday school story. It's so good to go back and learn from Daniel again and again. Even though Daniel's enemies, who were extremely jealous of him, convinced the king to write a law that said it was illegal for Daniel to pray to anyone other than the king of their time, King Darius, Daniel continued to pray to our one true God. And as punishment for breaking the law, he was thrown into a den of hungry lions. Talk about stressful times! But because Daniel never stopped praying, he was able to witness an amazing miracle—God shut the mouths of the lions so they didn't harm Daniel! And even more, the next day King Darius was so astonished by this miracle that he chose to believe in God and announced that all the people of his nation should too!

*Dear God, help me to have great courage like
Daniel, who never stopped praying to You
even when he was in great danger. Amen.*

REAL RICHES

"A rich man had a fertile farm that produced fine crops. He said to himself, 'What should I do? I don't have room for all my crops.' Then he said, 'I know! I'll tear down my barns and build bigger ones. Then I'll have room enough to store all my wheat and other goods. And I'll sit back and say to myself, "My friend, you have enough stored away for years to come. Now take it easy! Eat, drink, and be merry!" ' "But God said to him, 'You fool! You will die this very night. Then who will get everything you worked for?' "Yes, a person is a fool to store up earthly wealth but not have a rich relationship with God."

LUKE 12:16–21 NLT

❀

Jesus shared this parable to teach us that when we have a lot, we shouldn't worry much about saving it up. We should be willing to share it with others. No person has any idea exactly how long we will live on earth. It's far better to be generous to others than to selfishly store up everything we have. Our goal should be to have real riches that come from a close relationship with God, not the riches of this world.

Dear God, help me not to focus on storing up money and possessions. Please give me a heart that loves to share and draws closer and closer to You. Amen.

LET JESUS' TEACHING LIVE IN YOU

*Let the teaching of Christ and His words
keep on living in you. These make your
lives rich and full of wisdom.*
COLOSSIANS 3:16 NLV

Everything that we put into our minds through our eyes
and ears affects us. So, this scripture in Colossians 3
helps guide us. If we let all the teachings of Jesus and His
words actively live in us—meaning we focus on, listen to,
and obey them as we try our best to live like Jesus did—we
will have lives that are rich and full of wisdom. So, even
as you do something as simple as choosing your favorite
music, you can ask yourself, *Will this help me to focus
on God and following Jesus? If not, what can I choose instead that would help me focus on Him?*

*Dear God, please help me think about how
even the smallest choices in my life affect
my relationship with You. Amen.*

WHEN YOU'RE GRIEVING

*"God blesses those who mourn, for
they will be comforted."*
MATTHEW 5:4 NLT

If someone you love has died very suddenly, you know that it's an awful shock to lose someone with zero warning. Losing a loved one in any kind of way, whether you have a chance to say goodbye or not, is heartbreaking. But God gives special grace and care when we stay close to Him and let Him heal our broken hearts—even when we don't fully understand Him. We can stay close to Him through His Word and through prayer, crying out to Him with all our sadness, anger, fear, and confusion. And it's amazing how He will provide comfort in all kinds of ways.

If you are grieving the loss of a loved one, keep crying out to God and reading His Word. Tell Him everything you are feeling, and ask for His help. Search His Word, and let Him show you how He will heal your heart, providing His love in many ways.

*Dear God, please hold me extra close when I am
grieving and missing a loved one. I don't understand,
but I don't want to turn away from You. Please comfort
me, heal my heart, and grow my faith in You. Amen.*

PRAY THE NAMES OF GOD

*His name will be called Wonderful, Teacher, Powerful
God, Father Who Lives Forever, Prince of Peace.*
ISAIAH 9:6 NLV

Isaiah 9:6 gives some of the names of Jesus, and if you google "names of God," you'll find lists of scriptures pointing you to where you can find many more of His names in the Bible. Focusing on these names can be a powerful way to help you manage any worries and fears, because it helps you become aware of different aspects of our amazing God and the ways He cares for His beloved people.

Here are just a few of his wonderful names:

- Elohim means Creator God.

- Adonai means Master Over All.

- El Elyon means Most High God.

- Jehovah Jireh means the Lord Will Provide.

*Dear Elohim, my Creator God, You are Adonai, Master
Over All, including being Master over my life and every
challenge I face. You care about all my needs because
You are Jehovah Jireh and You will always provide!
Thank You, El Elyon, the Most High God! Amen.*

PUZZLING

Now we see things imperfectly, like puzzling reflections in a mirror, but then we will see everything with perfect clarity. All that I know now is partial and incomplete, but then I will know everything completely, just as God now knows me completely.
1 CORINTHIANS 13:12 NLT

Are you praying and asking God for answers but not understanding His ways? 1 Corinthians 13:12 is so important to remember. Everything in this world is messed up big-time from the perfect way God originally intended it, because sin entered the world when Adam and Eve chose to disobey Him. And the way we see things and try to understand is damaged because of sin too. But God is working out His plans, and at just the right time, He will make all things new and right. Then we will see things perfectly as He does, and it will be incredible!

Dear God, help me to trust You always, even when I'm so puzzled by what You're doing. Please give me peace that, at just the right time, You will make everything turn out right and good forever. Amen.

SPEND TIME IN THE PSALMS

*The Lord is near to all who call on Him, to all who
call on Him in truth. He will fill the desire of those
who fear Him. He will also hear their cry and will
save them. The Lord takes care of all who love Him.*
PSALM 145:18–20 NLV

Let the Bible be your go-to source of stress relief. Especially in the book of Psalms, you can read, pray, be encouraged, and soothed by all the poems, prayers, and praises to God. They are full of honest emotion as the writers pour out their hearts to God, and they can inspire you to do the same. There is nothing you need to hide from God. If you have sin in your life, confess it to Him and make things right. If you are hurting, tell God and let Him comfort you. If you or a loved one are in need, ask God for His help. If you are scared, let God remind you of His power and protection. If you are full of gratitude and praise, tell Him again and again!

*Dear God, help me to remember to turn to the psalms
often to be inspired and filled with peace. Amen.*

BEFORE YOU ASK HIM

*"Your Father knows exactly what you
need even before you ask him!"*
MATTHEW 6:8 NLT

❀

If God knows what we need before we even ask Him, like Matthew 6:8 says, then you might wonder, *Why should I even pray at all? God already knows!* Answer: Because God loves you *that* much! He wants a close relationship with you that much! He wants to hear from you even though He already knows everything about you and everything you need! The God of the whole universe wants to be close to you. Amazing! The fact that He already knows everything about you plus everything about *everything* is a reason to want to talk to Him even more; it's never a reason to think you don't need to bother praying!

*Dear God, You are my good and loving Father. You know
everything, and You already know exactly what I need
in every situation. I am amazed by Your greatness and
that You want to be close to me. Thank You! Amen.*

MIRACULOUS RESCUE

*So Peter was held in prison. But the
church kept praying to God for him.*
ACTS 12:5 NLV

Through reading God's Word, we can be reminded of
and encouraged by the many examples of God's work
in response to people's prayers. As the church kept on
praying for Peter while he was in prison, God moved to
rescue Peter in a miraculous way:

*The night before Peter was to be placed on trial, he was
asleep, fastened with two chains between two soldiers.
Others stood guard at the prison gate. Suddenly, there was
a bright light in the cell, and an angel of the Lord stood
before Peter. The angel struck him on the side to awaken
him and said, "Quick! Get up!" And the chains fell off his
wrists. Then the angel told him, "Get dressed and put on
your sandals." And he did. "Now put on your coat and follow
me," the angel ordered. So Peter left the cell, following the
angel. . . . "It's really true!" he said. "The Lord has sent his
angel and saved me from Herod and from what the Jewish
leader shad planned to do to me!" (Acts 12:6–9, 11 NLT).*

*Dear God, You're incredible! I trust that
You can certainly help me with any worry
or stress I'm dealing with! Amen.*

YOU ARE GIFTED

*In his grace, God has given us different
gifts for doing certain things well.*
ROMANS 12:6 NLT

God has given you special gifts and talents that He wants you to use to help spread His love and bring Him praise! When you're constantly asking God to show You His good plans and purposes for your life and then doing those things, you have little time and room in your mind for any worries. Maybe you have already figured out what some of your gifts are, and you might discover more as the years go by and you have new life experiences. Pray for God to give you confidence in the gifts He has given you, and ask Him for opportunities to share them well!

*Dear God, help me to realize all the gifts You've created
within me. Show me how You want me to use them to
point more people to knowing and loving You! Amen.*

TAKING GOOD CARE

*Physical training is of some value, but godliness
has value for all things, holding promise for
both the present life and the life to come.*
1 TIMOTHY 4:8 NIV

Some people become obsessed and worried about working out and getting in shape. It's an awesome goal to be fit and healthy, and 1 Corinthians 6:19–20 tells us we should want to take good care of our bodies and honor God with them. But physical fitness goals aren't awesome if people take them too far and give them too much attention. Our focus should be on God most of all. First Timothy 4:8 reminds us that growing in healthy relationship with Him—so that we do our best to live like Jesus—matters not just for life on earth, which is temporary, but for life in heaven, which is forever!

*Dear God, please help me keep my body healthy
and strong; but even more importantly, I want
to keep my heart, mind, and spirit in a healthy
and strong relationship with You! Amen.*

LOVE AND PRAY FOR THEM

"You have heard the law that says, 'Love your neighbor' and hate your enemy. But I say, love your enemies! Pray for those who persecute you!"
<small>MATTHEW 5:43–44 NLT</small>

If an enemy or even a "frenemy" is causing you worry and stress today, go to God's Word for a reminder to pray for that person. This scripture in Matthew 5 is a great example of how God's ways are often the opposite of our world's ways. It's popular and easy to love those who love you and to hate those who hate you. But that's not what God says to do, and it's sure not popular or easy to love and pray for the enemies in your life. Yet that's what God wants. It seems totally impossible sometimes! But with His help, we all can do it. It might be a huge struggle at first, but try it out and then keep trying! Watch how God blesses you when you obey His good commands and seek His help to love and pray for enemies.

Dear God, this good command of Yours is super hard to obey, and I sure can't do it on my own. But with Your help, I want to love and pray for my enemies. Amen.

PRAY THAT THEY WILL BE FILLED WITH LOVE

I pray that you will be filled with love. I pray that you will be able to understand how wide and how long and how high and how deep His love is. I pray that you will know the love of Christ. His love goes beyond anything we can understand. I pray that you will be filled with God Himself.

EPHESIANS 3:17–19 NLV

It's often true that the troubled and mean people in your life act terribly because they have so little love in their own lives. So, as you're praying for enemies and "frenemies," this prayer in Ephesians 3 is a great place to start. Of course, you can and should pray for friends and loved ones too. But if you pray this way for enemies, who knows how God might completely transform their hearts? God can do anything!

Dear God, please fill my enemies and frenemies up to overflowing with Your love. Help me show Your love to them however they need, however You want me to. Amen.

BE HUMBLE

*Pride brings a person low, but the
lowly in spirit gain honor.*
PROVERBS 29:23 NIV

Pride gets us into a lot of trouble and causes a lot of our stress and anxiety. We should want to be humble not prideful. That means we admit our sin and mistakes. It means we don't think of ourselves as better than other people. It means we are teachable, knowing we can always keep learning from others and never trying to be know-it-alls. It doesn't mean we can't have any confidence or be happy with our accomplishments, but as humble Christians, we'll place our confidence in God's work within us, recognizing that He alone gives us the ability to accomplish any good thing!

*Dear God, in a world where it's not usually the
cool thing to be and do, I want to always be able
to admit my sin and mistakes and be teachable. I
want to give You credit and praise for everything.
Please help me with this all my life. Amen.*

MAKE THE BEST USE OF YOUR TIME

*So be careful how you live. Live as men who are wise
and not foolish. Make the best use of your time.*
EPHESIANS 5:15–16 NLV

Are you wise about how much time you spend on your phone and social media? Do you regularly choose to put down your phone and do things without a screen? Do you encourage your friends to do so as well? You can read books. You can play board games. You can get involved in sports and activities. You can spend time talking in person and just hanging out together. You can do all kinds of things people did before smartphones were ever invented! All these things can help reduce worry and anxiety in your life. Challenge yourself to see how much fun you can have with no phone or social media involved—and let that fun motivate you to set healthy limits.

*Dear God, I want to be wise about my phone and
social media and make the best use of my time like
Your Word tells me to. Please help me. Amen.*

GOD'S PROTECTION

The first time I was brought before the judge, no one
came with me. Everyone abandoned me. May it not
be counted against them. But the Lord stood with
me and gave me strength so that I might preach
the Good News in its entirety for all the Gentiles to
hear. And he rescued me from certain death. Yes,
and the Lord will deliver me from every evil attack
and will bring me safely into his heavenly Kingdom.
2 Timothy 4:16–18 nlt

Anytime you might feel alone or abandoned, you can read
and remember these words from Paul in the Bible. Even
with no one else there to help, God Himself was with
Paul and protected him and gave him power. And Paul
trusted that God would keep away every bad plan that
people had against him. Paul also knew that no matter
what happened on earth, God would someday bring him
into heaven forever.

Dear God, thank You for Your protection. I
trust that no matter what happens here in
this world, You will ultimately keep me safe,
because someday You are going to bring me into
perfect paradise in heaven with You! Amen.

LET'S KEEP LOOKING TO JESUS

*Let us put every thing out of our lives that keeps
us from doing what we should. Let us keep running
in the race that God has planned for us. Let us
keep looking to Jesus. Our faith comes from Him
and He is the One Who makes it perfect.*

HEBREWS 12:1–2 NLV

Sometimes we worry that we're missing out. There are
so many cool things to do in life, but we sure can't do
them all. It's just not possible! So, we need God's help to
choose the best things He has for us amid the many good
things. (And there are lots of not-good things to stay far
away from too.) The best way to live is to keep looking to
Jesus, keep reading His Word, keep praying to Him and
asking Him to show you the race God has mapped out
specifically for you.

*Dear Jesus, I want to keep looking to You and
following Your example. Please keep showing me the
good race God has mapped out for me. Amen.*

THE SUN AND MOON STOOD STILL

*On the day the LORD gave the Israelites victory
over the Amorites, Joshua prayed to the LORD
in front of all the people of Israel. He said, "Let
the sun stand still over Gibeon, and the moon
over the valley of Aijalon." So the sun stood still
and the moon stayed in place until the nation
of Israel had defeated its enemies. . . . There
has never been a day like this one before or
since, when the LORD answered such a prayer.*

JOSHUA 10:12–14 NLT

This is such an incredible story to remember when you're
praying for God to help ease your worries. Joshua prayed
for the sun and moon to stand still to give extra daylight
so God's people could win the war against their enemies,
the Amorites. And God answered in a way He had never
done before and has never done again. Clearly, God can
do absolutely anything, so He can certainly calm your
anxiety. He can help you with every one of your needs,
as well as those of your family and friends!

*Dear God, please remind me constantly of Your
all-powerful ways! No problem or worry or
fear I have is ever too big for You! Amen.*

A LOVE FOR LEARNING

Show me your ways, LORD, teach me your paths.
Guide me in your truth and teach me,
for you are God my Savior, and my
hope is in you all day long.
PSALM 25:4–5 NIV

Learning is not just something we do at school. Every day of your life, you can wake up asking God, "Will You please teach me today?" And in every situation, whether good or bad, you can ask, "God, what do You want me to learn from this?" And you can repeat those prayers all throughout your day.

You can let God teach you through your teachers, classes, and experiences at school. You can listen and learn from other people's experiences. You can read good books and glean information from trustworthy sources and seek out wisdom from others. Most importantly, you can keep learning from God's Word and right teaching at church and from other believers who are strong in their faith.

Dear God, please help me never stop learning
and loving to learn. You created my beautiful
mind and made it capable of so much. Help
me to use it for Your glory. Amen.

OVER IT

When I am afraid, I put my trust in you.
In God, whose word I praise—
in God I trust and am not afraid.
PSALM 56:3–4 NIV

Can you think of a fear or worry you used to have, but then you got over it? What happened? How did God help you? Who were the people and things He provided to get you through it? Every once in a while, it's good to take time to think about things you used to be afraid of that now seem like no big deal. It helps you realize that whatever is making you anxious today will probably be no big deal sometime in the future. God never leaves you alone. He is right there with you in the middle of your fears, and you can call out for His help at any time. He will guide you through it to the other side, where you can look back with relief and say, "Wow! Thanks, God! We conquered that together, and now I'm not worried about it anymore!"

Dear God, I remember all the ways You have helped
me conquer worries and fears in the past, and I
am trusting that You will help again. Amen.

BE SALT AND LIGHT

*"You are the salt of the earth. If salt loses its taste,
how can it be made to taste like salt again? . . . You
are the light of the world. . . . Let your light shine in
front of men. Then they will see the good things you
do and will honor your Father Who is in heaven."*
MATTHEW 5:13–14, 16 NLV

Sometimes you might worry about sharing your faith in
Jesus. You might feel like it's best to stay mostly quiet
about it. But that's exactly what our enemy Satan wants
you to think. Jesus said we should want to be like salt and
light. Salt helps food taste its best, and we should want
to bring out the best in others and help show them life at
its very best. Life at its best is a life that believes in and
follows Jesus. Jesus also wants us to be the light of the
world. If we hide our light, we can't help others see the
way to Jesus. But if we shine our light, giving Him honor
through every good thing we do, we help others honor
Him too.

*Dear God, I don't want to worry about sharing my faith.
I want to reach out to others and be salt and light to
them, helping them know and love Jesus too! Amen.*

STRONGER FAITH

"Lord, I have faith. Help my weak faith to be stronger!"
MARK 9:24 NLV

If you ever struggle to understand what God is doing or not doing about what you're praying for, think about a story in the Bible from Mark 9. A father was asking Jesus for help for his son, and it was so hard for the man to imagine that Jesus could do what he was asking. The father said to Jesus, "Have mercy on us and help us, if you can." Jesus replied, "What do you mean, 'If I can'? . . . Anything is possible if a person believes" (Mark 9:22–23 NLT). And the father said, "Lord, I have faith. Help my weak faith to be stronger!"

When you pray, remember that God can do exactly what you ask and so much more! He may or may not answer the way you want, but no matter how God responds to your prayer, your main response to God should be "Lord, I have faith. Help my weak faith to be stronger!"

Dear God, thank You that I can ask You for more and more faith. I believe anything is possible with You. I want to be stronger in my faith each day! Amen.

PRAYER FOR OUR PROTECTORS

*"No one can have greater love than
to give his life for his friends."*
JOHN 15:13 NLV

Following the news about crime can cause lots of worry and anxiety. Do you have any family members or friends who serve in the military or on a police force? Think of ways to honor and encourage them—like taking food to your local police station, sending cards and packages to service members who are overseas, and always thanking a person in military uniform for their service. Most importantly, you can pray for their safety as they work to keep others safe and free. Especially pray that each one would know Jesus as their Savior!

*Dear God, those who work in the armed forces
and police forces are so brave and give so much to
others, knowing at any time their life could be taken
as they work to protect others. Please bless, help,
and protect them in extra-special ways. Amen.*

KNOW YOUR ENEMY

Keep awake! Watch at all times. The devil is working against you. He is walking around like a hungry lion with his mouth open. He is looking for someone to eat. Stand against him and be strong in your faith.
1 PETER 5:8–9 NLV

We have an enemy, the devil, who is like a hungry lion lurking around with his mouth open, ready to destroy us. Realizing that and thinking about it is not fun, but it's better to know our enemy than pretend he doesn't exist. If we act like he's not real, we won't be prepared to watch out for him and his attacks. But we can stand strong against the devil by standing strong in our faith in the one true God and our Savior Jesus Christ. And we don't ever have to live in fear and anxiety, because God is always greater and more powerful (1 John 4) than anything the devil tries to do.

Dear God, please strengthen my faith in You. I want to be close in relationship and obedience to You so I can stand strong against the enemy, who wants to destroy me. Amen.

GATHER TOGETHER TO PRAY

*"For where two or three are gathered together
in My name, there I am with them."*
MATTHEW 18:20 NLV

Do you have friends or family members with whom you share needs and concerns and worries? Do you also spend time together praying about those things? If not, start today by initiating a regular prayer time with your family. While at church or school or your activities, offer to pray for your friends, and ask them to pray for you too. Find efficient and effective ways and times to spend time together in prayer. Prayer is always powerful, and gathering together to support each other and join in corporate prayer brings about more of the benefits and power of prayer.

*Dear God, thank You for family and friends and
the times when we gather so we can all talk to
You together! These times are so encouraging,
and I want to make them a habit. Amen.*

COMFORT

*Praise be to the God and Father of our Lord Jesus
Christ, the Father of compassion and the God of
all comfort, who comforts us in all our troubles, so
that we can comfort those in any trouble with the
comfort we ourselves receive from God. For just as
we share abundantly in the sufferings of Christ, so
also our comfort abounds through Christ. If we are
distressed, it is for your comfort and salvation; if we
are comforted, it is for your comfort, which produces in
you patient endurance of the same sufferings we suffer.*
2 CORINTHIANS 1:3–6 NIV

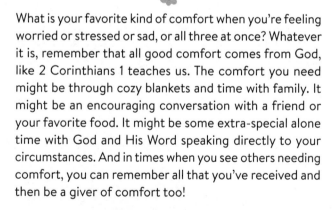

What is your favorite kind of comfort when you're feeling
worried or stressed or sad, or all three at once? Whatever
it is, remember that all good comfort comes from God,
like 2 Corinthians 1 teaches us. The comfort you need
might be through cozy blankets and time with family. It
might be an encouraging conversation with a friend or
your favorite food. It might be some extra-special alone
time with God and His Word speaking directly to your
circumstances. And in times when you see others needing
comfort, you can remember all that you've received and
then be a giver of comfort too!

*Dear God, thank You so much for all the comfort You
provide. Help me to share it generously! Amen.*

PRAY FOR YOUR CHURCH

Those who believed what Peter said were baptized
and added to the church that day—about 3,000
in all. All the believers devoted themselves to the
apostles' teaching, and to fellowship, and to sharing
in meals (including the Lord's Supper), and to prayer.
ACTS 2:41–42 NLT

If you belong to a local church, you have a group of people who are your church family, who need your love and support as they give you love and support too. They all need your prayer as well. Every time you walk in the doors of your church, you can pray for the protection of your church and the people who come. You can pray for the pastor and leaders and teachers and employees and volunteers. You can pray for your church to preach and follow God's Word and glorify Him in everything. You can pray God brings more and more people to your church to hear His truth and experience His love.

Dear God, I pray for my church family and all those
who need to come to my church to learn more
about You. I pray that You would help me to serve
and be active in my church all my life. Amen.

TEAMWORK

*"May they experience such perfect unity that
the world will know that you sent me and that
you love them as much as you love me."*
JOHN 17:23 NLT

Good teamwork is necessary in a lot of areas of life. You've probably experienced this in sports or group projects at school. But it can also be very hard for people to work together well! Did you know Jesus specifically prayed for good teamwork among Christians? He prayed for unity, that all His followers through all of time would be one team with God, the Father, and Jesus, the Son, working together to share God's love and help more and more people believe in Jesus. Here is Jesus' prayer in John 17:20–21, 23 (NLT):

"I am praying not only for these disciples but also for all who will ever believe in me through their message. I pray that they will all be one, just as you and I are one—as you are in me, Father, and I am in you. And may they be in us so that the world will believe you sent me. . . . May they experience such perfect unity that the world will know that you sent me and that you love them as much as you love me."

Dear God, please help me with teamwork in school and activities, and also help me to promote good teamwork among Jesus-followers so that we can win at sharing Your love and truth. Amen.

GOD CARES ABOUT EVERY SORROW

You keep track of all my sorrows. You have collected all my tears in your bottle.

PSALM 56:8 NLT

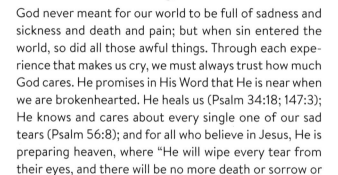

God never meant for our world to be full of sadness and sickness and death and pain; but when sin entered the world, so did all those awful things. Through each experience that makes us cry, we must always trust how much God cares. He promises in His Word that He is near when we are brokenhearted. He heals us (Psalm 34:18; 147:3); He knows and cares about every single one of our sad tears (Psalm 56:8); and for all who believe in Jesus, He is preparing heaven, where "He will wipe every tear from their eyes, and there will be no more death or sorrow or crying or pain. All these things are gone forever" (Revelation 21:4 NLT).

When you are hurting, pray to God. Cry to Him. Let Him collect your tears. Focus on the truth of these scriptures. He will help you keep going and finding joy, and one day He will make everything right.

Dear God, thank You for caring about every tear I cry. I trust You and want to follow You no matter what. Amen.

JUST SPEAK THE WORD, JESUS

"Only speak the word, and my servant will be healed."
MATTHEW 8:8 NLV

When we pray, we need to remember the example of the army captain in the book of Matthew in the Bible. He had such great faith that Jesus only had to say the word and his servant would be healed:

Jesus came to the city of Capernaum. A captain of the army came to Him. He asked for help, saying, "Lord, my servant is sick in bed. He is not able to move his body. He is in much pain." Jesus said to the captain, "I will come and heal him." The captain said, "Lord, I am not good enough for You to come to my house. Only speak the word, and my servant will be healed."... When Jesus heard this, He was surprised and wondered about it. He said to those who followed Him, "For sure, I tell you, I have not found so much faith in the Jewish nation"... Jesus said to the captain, "Go your way. It is done for you even as you had faith to believe." The servant was healed at that time (Matthew 8:5–8, 10, 13 NLV).

Dear God, please grow my faith in You to be as strong as this army captain's faith. I know You can just say the word and make a miracle happen! Amen.

GOD WON'T CHANGE

*Jesus Christ is the same yesterday
and today and forever.*
HEBREWS 13:8 NLV

Big change in our lives, or even lots of little change all at once, can cause worry and stress. What ways have you experienced stress because of changes? What were your thoughts, emotions, and prayers like during that time? Nothing in life will always stay the same, and that's why we can be so thankful that God gave us Jesus, who is always dependable and always the same—yesterday, today, and forever! Psalm 102:25–27 (NLV) says of God, "You made the earth in the beginning. You made the heavens with Your hands. They will be destroyed but You will always live. They will all become old as clothing becomes old. You will change them like a coat. And they will be changed, but You are always the same. Your years will never end."

God is *never* going to let us down. So, lean on Him and ask Him to hold you steady when life seems to swirl around you with new circumstances. Talk to Him about every joy and sorrow and stress.

*Dear God, thank You for never changing or letting
me down through all life's ups and downs! Amen.*

A SUDDEN SITUATION

Be strong in the Lord and in his mighty power.
EPHESIANS 6:10 NLT

❀

Sometimes in life we are unexpectedly thrown into things we don't know how to do. Can you think of a time when that kind of thing has happened to you? Sometimes God lets that happen on purpose so we can get over our fears and worries and so He can show us how we can depend on Him for His help. He is always there, and we can always call on Him in prayer. We might be surprised at what we are capable of with His power working in us!

Dear God, sometimes I find myself suddenly in a situation where I don't have a clue what to do! Help me to realize how much I can depend on You and Your power in those times. Teach me what You want me to learn, and strengthen me in my faith, please, God! Amen.

HEAVENLY MINDED

Keep your minds thinking about things in heaven.
COLOSSIANS 3:2 NLV

God has wonderful plans for your life here on earth! Ephesians 2:10 (NLT) says, "We are God's masterpiece. He has created us anew in Christ Jesus, so we can do the good things he planned for us long ago." But God doesn't want us to get too attached to our lives here on earth because they are not our forever lives with Him in heaven. First John 2:15, 17 (NLT) says, "Do not love this world nor the things it offers you. . . . This world is fading away, along with everything that people crave. But anyone who does what pleases God will live forever." We need to keep the good perspective of finding joy and purpose in the plans for which God has created us while remembering that our life on earth is temporary and our forever home is in heaven.

Dear God, thank You for the good plans You created me for here on earth. Help me to walk closely with You and do the things You want me to do for Your glory. And thank You that someday I will live forever in perfect heaven! Amen.

TESTS AND MORE TESTS

Dear friends, your faith is going to be tested as if it were going through fire. Do not be surprised at this.
1 PETER 4:12 NLV

❀

Tests at school aren't just the typical ones you first think of. Of course, there are the regular kinds of tests to see what you know, but you also have tests of your faith at school. There will always be difficult challenges and people to deal with, and you'll be tested on how you handle these situations. Will you pray and let God help in each one? Will you avoid pressure to do things you know are wrong? Will you reach out in kindness to the classmate others are picking on? All of these are opportunities to prove and grow your faith.

During these tests, the Bible says you are to "be happy that you are able to share some of the suffering of Christ. When His shining-greatness is shown, you will be filled with much joy. If men speak bad of you because you are a Christian, you will be happy because the Spirit of shining-greatness and of God is in you" (1 Peter 4:13–14 NLV).

Dear God, help me to see every kind of test as a chance to prove and show my faith in You. Please help me to ace all the tests of my faith. Amen.

LET YOUR LOVE GROW MORE AND MORE

*And this is my prayer: I pray that your
love will grow more and more.*
PHILIPPIANS 1:9 NLV

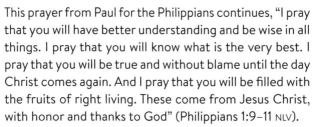

This prayer from Paul for the Philippians continues, "I pray that you will have better understanding and be wise in all things. I pray that you will know what is the very best. I pray that you will be true and without blame until the day Christ comes again. And I pray that you will be filled with the fruits of right living. These come from Jesus Christ, with honor and thanks to God" (Philippians 1:9–11 NLV).

We can copy this prayer because it applies to *all* believers of Jesus. And all believers can pray it for each other too. Healthy, true Christians won't ever want to stop growing in love and in understanding of God and His Word—and as we do, our worries and fears will be relieved.

*Dear God, like Paul prayed, I want to have love
that grows more and more; I want to have better
understanding and be wise in all things; I want
to know what is best; I want to be true and
blameless; I want to be filled with the fruits that
come from living right. I know all good things
come from You, and I praise You! Amen.*

WHEN IT'S GOOD TO FEEL BAD

*Cling to your faith in Christ, and keep your
conscience clear. For some people have
deliberately violated their consciences; as a
result, their faith has been shipwrecked.*
1 TIMOTHY 1:19 NLT

Sometimes worry and anxiety fill us because of sin we're
holding on to and not confessing and asking forgiveness
like we need to. Because He loves us so much, God sometimes purposefully gives us bad feelings inside through His
Holy Spirit. Those feelings, as a reminder to confess sin,
are a whole lot better than letting lies and sin get bigger
and bigger—and out of control—in our lives. Usually, as
soon as we admit and confess the sin and ask forgiveness,
the anxiety we were feeling is gone. We should pray, all
the time, that we feel the good kinds of worry and anxiety
that motivate us to admit our sins and make them right.

*Dear God, please help me to choose to live by Your
Word. But when I do mess up, I want to feel bad about
choosing to sin and then holding on to it. Help me
to admit and confess my sins and ask forgiveness
quickly every time. Thank You for Your grace! Amen.*

GOD IS FAITHFUL AND JUST, HE FORGIVES AND PURIFIES

*If we claim to be without sin, we deceive ourselves
and the truth is not in us. If we confess our sins,
he is faithful and just and will forgive us our
sins and purify us from all unrighteousness.*
1 JOHN 1:8–9 NIV

Even after we pray to confess sin and have asked forgiveness from God and anyone we've hurt, sometimes we keep feeling awful for what we did wrong. But God promises time and again in His Word that we shouldn't. He takes our sins as far as the east is from the west (Psalm 103:11–12)! And, if God doesn't hold our sin against us, why on earth should we?

Our enemy, Satan, wants us to focus on our mistakes and beat ourselves up so that we feel defeated and useless. So, pray against the enemy, and believe in the power of Jesus to forgive you and take away your sin completely!

*Dear God, when I confess my sin, You want me to feel
relieved, forgiven, and free from it! I trust that You
love and forgive perfectly and completely! Amen.*

HOLY SPIRIT SUPERPOWER

"The Holy Spirit is coming. He will lead you into all truth. He will not speak His Own words. He will speak what He hears. He will tell you of things to come."

JOHN 16:13 NLV

Our worries are so often about what "could" happen to us. It would be nice to have a superpower to be able to see into the future, warning us of danger and bad situations and helping us to make choices that will bring us only good things. And in a way, all of us who have the Holy Spirit because we believe in Jesus (Romans 8) *do* have a superpower. So, we can pray like this:

Dear God, I can't see into the future, but I know You can. I need Your Holy Spirit in me to warn me of danger and situations that would be bad for me. Please raise red flags and help me sense Your direction away from what is harmful for me. Point me toward what is good for me, according to Your will. I don't need to be worried or afraid of the future; I simply need to trust and depend on You, Your power, Your perfect plans, and Your love. Amen.

SCRIPTURE INDEX

Old Testament

New Testament

MORE ENCOURAGEMENT FOR YOUR BEAUTIFUL SPIRIT!

You Belong
Devotions and Prayers for a Teen Girl's Heart

This delightful devotional is a lovely reminder of that you were created with purpose by a heavenly Creator. . .and that you belong—right here and now—in this world. 180 encouraging readings and inspiring prayers, rooted in biblical truth, will reassure your uncertain heart, helping you to understand that you're never alone and always loved. In each devotional reading, you will encounter the bountiful blessings and grace of your Creator, while coming to trust His purposeful plan for you in this world.

Flexible Casebound / 978-1-63609-169-3